A College Grows in Oregon

A College Grows in Oregon

The Splendid Audacity of Pacific University

Marion F. Giersbach

BEE ☗ TREE

PACIFIC UNIVERSITY LIBRARIES
Forest Grove, Oregon

ISBN 978-0-9884827-7-7

Published by Pacific University Libraries 2016

Estate of Marion F. Giersbach
Walter F. Giersbach, Executor
11 Nottingham Lane
Manchester, NJ 08759

Pacific University Libraries
2043 College Way
Forest Grove, Oregon 97116

www.pacificu.edu/libraries

Bee Tree Books
An imprint of the Pacific University Libraries

Our treasure lies in the beehive of our knowledge. We are perpetually on the way thither, being by nature [...] honey gatherers of the mind.
Friedrich Nietzsche

The "Bee Tree", an iconic ivy-covered tree that stood on the Pacific University campus for many years, was already old and hollow when pioneer Tabitha Brown arrived in Oregon in 1846. Mrs. Brown started a home for orphans that would grow into Pacific University. According to the Forest Grove *News-Times*, the tree was "said to have housed a swarm of bees who furnished the little old lady with honey which she sold to buy provisions for her orphan children."

Table of Contents

"The ultimate purpose and hope is seen in the provision making it possible for a collegiate department to be established whenever it seemed feasible. In this provision for collegiate education it preceded all educational institutions on the Pacific Coast. It may be regarded as one of the acts of Splendid Audacity with which the student of western history becomes familiar."

James Rood Robertson
Origin of Pacific University, 1905

Acknowledgements

There are so many who have contributed to my research that I must express my great thanks: To the directors of the Oregon Historical Society, Portland, for their files: the Alvin Smith diaries, notes by author Eva Emery Dye, copies of the American Board Letters (1836-42) and the Oregon Quarterlies; The American Board Archives, Houghton Library (Boston); the Bancroft Library in Berkeley, California, with its collection of early-day manuscripts of the settlers; the Huntington Library in San Marino, California, and the assistants who helped on my many visits to locate manuscripts; the Oberlin College Treasury department and the Oberlin College Library; the Quincy (Illinois) Public Library and the Quincy Congregational Church; the University of Missouri Library, Columbia, Missouri; the Indian Affairs Archives in Washington, D.C. and our Oregon representatives in Congress who came to my aid; the Chicago Theological Seminary, which houses the American Home Missionary material; Pacific University, Forest Grove, Oregon, for early trustee reports and the Library for manuscript material of the early days and the Griffin papers; all the sons and daughters of the pioneers who gave their time and memories—the Platts, George Durham, with Emeline Clark's album, Margaret Hinman, Mrs. H.A. Lewis and James Wheelock Marsh.

There are many others who sent suggestions and letters, and all of these deserve my added thanks. As I recently went over the years of correspondence, I became aware of how many people added their bits to this chronicle. I must not forget my husband, Dr. Walter C. Giersbach, who searched willingly on our library visits, or Mrs. Lyndall Richards, who has been my conscience since our days together in Forest Grove.

Marion F. Giersbach, August 1991

Preface

It was my good fortune to arrive in the Oregon country in 1941, while the children and grandchildren of the pioneers were still alive and living in Forest Grove, Portland, the Willamette Valley and, particularly, the Tualatin Plains in northwest Oregon.

One of my choicest and dearest friends was Wheelock Marsh, the elder son of Sidney Harper Marsh, first president of Pacific University, who shared a lifetime of reminiscences with me. Another was Margaret Hinman, whose grandfather, Alanson Hinman, worked with Jason Lee and settled in the Tualatin area. There were also two grandsons of Rev. Harvey and Emeline Clark, George Durham and Harrison Platt, and a great granddaughter, Helen Platt. Included, too, were grandchildren of Rev. Elkanah and Mary Walker, missionaries in 1839 to the Indians with Dr. Marcus Whitman. They came to the West Plain after the Whitman massacre. And the descendants of Tabitha Brown, who mothered orphan students in 1847.

There were some who took me on trips over the back roads so I might have a sense of the location of Dairy Creek in the North Tualatin Plain, and how people traveled the trail between Hillsboro, Cornelius and Forest Grove in the early days.

One of the most elusive individuals in my research was Rev. Harvey Clark of Chester, Vermont. Born in 1807, he was one of the Clark brothers, stone masons, who built many of the stone houses in North Chester and the Cavendish area. As he worked quarrying and laying the stone, he had time to think, and he decided he did not want to be a stone mason all his life. A friend shook his head and said, "What a pity, to lose a fine stone mason to an indifferent ministry."[1]

Mr. Clark and his wife came west with the American Fur Traders in 1840. He became a preacher, organized two churches, taught the Indians and then the white children. But there were few details and large gaps in

---

1   *Oregon Historical Quarterly.*

his early years before arriving on Tualatin Plains. As a Pacific University professor, James Rood Robertson, wrote in 1905, "There is not much to be found in the form of written record concerning Mr. Clark, but his place in the community was a large one."

My curiosity was such that I set out to find all I could about this man and his wife, Emeline. What was the driving power that led them, in spite of hardships and poverty, to stay with their mission year after year, to build a world of which they could be proud?

I give great credit not only to the children of the pioneers for their help, but to my husband and sons who encouraged me constantly. They became as interested in the project as I was, and without argument traveled the Oregon Trail many times, stopping to check libraries and historical societies along the way for pertinent material.

This has now become a story of more than one man. It incorporates the lives of many: their dreams, their struggles and disappointments, the legacy they left for future generations. There is good reason that some of their names are in the rotunda of the Capitol in Salem. It is important that we pass on our history to the next generation. Only in this way can we keep the records straight as to what happened, when and why, and who the founders were in building each phase of this great state of Oregon.

Introduction to the Oregon Country

To appreciate those who built the West, we must understand the beginnings which created the urge to acquire this new land. If you are a longtime student of Oregon history, such a recital will be repetitive. If you are embarking on this segment of early history as a neophyte, a reminder of how it all evolved will be helpful, even in capsule form. And, if your curiosity is really aroused, there are many volumes with exciting details to whet your appetite.

The Oregon country received its earliest notices in the East when it was reported that Capt. Robert Gray, an American from Boston coming by sea, discovered and laid claim to the Columbia River and its tributaries in May 1792. Capt. Gray had heard that the Spanish had reported that there was a large river in the area, but it had not been found. Gray, who was financed by a group of merchants in Boston to sail new waters and find trade for them, explored up the river a distance of 25 miles. Although he was not an explorer, curiosity had made it possible for him to find the Columbia.

Later that same year, George Vancouver, a British subject, sailed to the Columbia and left his lieutenant, Broughton, to explore the river with a smaller vessel while he returned to San Francisco. Broughton went about 100 miles upriver, giving names to peaks he saw and areas he passed. The last spot they passed before turning down river he called Point Vancouver. The findings of Gray and Broughton raised a question to plague both the United States and Great Britain: which country really saw the Columbia first and might lay claim to the territory?

President Jefferson heartily believed in expansion. After the Louisiana Purchase had been made, he sent Lewis and Clark on an exploratory trip to the West Coast in great secrecy, hoping Britain would not hear about it. The Lewis and Clark party made a very thorough study of what they found, with detailed reports, charting of rivers, types of Indians they encountered, kinds of geography and possibilities for expansion. President Jefferson felt that this, added to Gray's discovery of the Columbia, gave the United States an added advantage. However, word of the Lewis and Clark expedition leaked out, and the British Northwest Company, rival to the Hudson's Bay

Company, began to set up trading posts at planned locations toward the Columbia River.

In 1811, the Astors of New York were successful in establishing the American Fur Company on the south side of the Columbia at the mouth of the river. They represented American interests. Before too many years passed, the Northwest Company forced out the Astors and bought the American Fur Company.

During this period of rivalry between the fur companies, Dr. John McLoughlin, a Canadian, educated as a physician, became a partner in the Northwest Company. Shortly thereafter, the Northwest Company merged with the Hudson's Bay Company. In 1824, John McLoughlin established the most western outpost of the British at Fort Vancouver. He had become head factor, which gave him great decision-making power. He laid out 3,000 acres of land, and a sizeable fort was built in 1825. He became an absolute, but benevolent, head of his "government", respected by both Indians and trappers or traders who worked with him.

The professional trappers found beavers and other fur-bearing animals in plentiful supply, and the fur trade flourished. Those in the East and in other countries could use all the furs they could get, and beaver hats were particularly popular. These same trappers and traders unknowingly held a unique position in the development of the Oregon country, joining the mission families and scattered settlers as they came west.

Oregon is unique for another reason, as the only region added to the United States by discovery, exploration and occupation. Alaska and Louisiana were purchased, and California was won in a war with Mexico. But no money changed hands, nor had war entered the picture, when the Oregon Territory became a part of the United States.[1]

And in still another way the Oregon country is unique; it was the most ignored by the United States government, which turned a deaf ear to the calls for guidance from settlers.

The years from 1818-46 saw joint occupancy with Great Britain. Until a time was ripe to talk about boundaries, both countries thought it was well to avoid conflict as long as possible. McLoughlin at Vancouver kept things under control with both whites and Indians.

While the mountain men were often described as earthy and uncouth, it is well known that many of them had come from "pious homes" in the East, and were well-educated according to the standards of the day. One of

---

1   *Oregon General Histories* and varied sources.

these early trappers and explorers, Jedediah Smith, carried his Bible with him wherever he went. Another, Osborne Russell, hunted furs, but between hunting seasons he camped near one of the forts so he could borrow books.

As these men traveled about, they learned enough Indian jargon so they could converse with the natives. They described their homes and life "back east" and even explained about the Bibles they read on the trail. They noted that Indians seemed impressed by the story of the Christian God.

While history was being made in the West by these mountain men, reports came to the East about the River of the West, the Lewis and Clark expedition, the Astors. Eastern writers began to examine the possibilities available. One of these people was the poet William Cullen Bryant, whose "Thanatopsis" was printed in September 1817 in the *North American Review*: "Take the wings / Of morning, pierce the Barcan wilderness, or lose thyself in the continuous woods / Where rolls the Oregon, and leaves no sounds."

Also in 1817, a Boston school teacher, Hall Kelley, became enthusiastic about the new land to the west—so enthusiastic that he became obsessed with the subject, reading everything he could find. By 1820, he had published and distributed many pamphlets about Oregon. He also wrote memorials, which he sent to Congress, advising them to advance money to help settle the Oregon country. Congress ignored him, but he kept pushing for his cause. He incorporated "The American Society for Encouraging the Settlement of the Oregon Country." In 1831, he prepared a circular for emigrants, even though he had never been west, nor was he familiar with the conditions first hand.

In fact, in 1829, using his fertile imagination and such maps as he could find, Kelley drew up a plan for a city in Oregon. He felt the most likely place for a settlement should be between the Columbia and the Willamette Rivers. His plan was never followed, we are told, although Portland later became a reality in that vicinity. The water power available at Wallamut Falls, later to become Oregon City, and its location on the trails west made *it* the most natural place for early settlement.[2]

Kelley's ideas may not have had any effect on Congress, but they did bear fruit. One individual who responded was Nathaniel Wyeth of Cambridge, Massachusetts. He read Hall Kelley's treatises avidly, and intended to meet a ship that he had dispatched with trade goods for the Indians. The ship was lost at sea, so Wyeth returned east and loaded a second vessel

---

2   *Ibid.*

which did meet him on his arrival at the Columbia in 1834. This time, Wyeth set up a trading post on the Willamette River.

Another man, who made a greater impact on the settlement of Oregon, was Rev. Jason Lee, a Methodist minister who, according to one source, said his first knowledge of Oregon came through Hall Kelley. In 1831, four young Indians had also journeyed to St. Louis with fur traders from the West, commissioned by their chief to seek men who would come and tell them about the Christian God. In 1834, Jason Lee and his son, Daniel, arrived in the Oregon territory to bring the Christian God to the Indians.

Hall Kelley's efforts had brought positive results. He had been instrumental in the beginnings, feeble though they were, of Oregon's settlement by Americans. Did Kelley ever see Oregon with his own eyes? Yes, he actually made the trip in 1834, going south through Mexico and into California. Here he looked for people going north to Oregon. He met Ewing Young, who we will meet later, and several other young men, and suggested they go north together. An estimated 16 people made up the party; one of them was Young, another was Joseph Gale,[3] who later became prominent in the Portland area. Kelley, though, did not stay long. In 1835, he returned to Massachusetts, never to see Oregon again. But he continued to write and talk about Oregon until his death in 1874.

This is the base upon which the Oregon country expanded and became the westernmost outpost of the United States. It is also the story of the unrecognized heroes who followed the traders: Jason Lee, Marcus Whitman and others who built the west with their life blood. Many have been forgotten over the years, yet in their struggles they were instrumental in laying the firm foundations for religion, education and government in the vast Oregon Territory.

---

3   *Ibid.*

Chapter 1
Dreams

OBERLIN COLLEGIATE INSTITUTE, OHIO, 1837-38

It was a bright spring day in 1839, and Oberlin had never looked lovelier to the young couple standing beside their horse and wagon. The college town had been home for two exciting years, and the students with them had become their friends during that time. There were only a few buildings, mingled with the settlers' cabins on the campus so recently hewn out of the Ohio wilderness. The founders of the young college had brought a sense of mission and integrity to their students. Today's departure of one such couple represented their zeal for mission and service, for Harvey Clark and Emeline Cadwell were going west to minister to the Indians in strange country, and their student friends were there to wish them Godspeed.

A few months earlier, a fellow student, John Griffin, had left the campus for the West. Now Harvey Clark looked forward to meeting the Griffin party in Independence, Missouri, in time to join the American Fur Brigade on the Oregon Trail.

The light spring wagon, loaded with the basics that Harvey and Emeline had procured for the trip, was ready. The horse was eager to be off, and finally they were on their way. They settled back in the seat with sighs of relief. It had taken longer than they had expected to get financial help for their trip, and they admitted they were impatient at the delays. But at last they were on the road to Independence and a future with the Indians in the far west as they had dreamed.

Harvey smiled at Emeline, and received an answering grin of appreciation. Harvey was a tall young man, thin but muscular and strong. His hair was dark and hung to his shoulders. While his complexion was weather-dark, he was smooth-shaven, and one was aware of the intent expression in his blue eyes as he listened to what people had to say. He was equally good at asking questions when he wanted to learn about unfamiliar situations.

Emeline was a contrast to Harvey. She was younger than he was, smaller of bone, lissome with a merry smile, and was usually a very demure miss unless she was bothered; then her reaction would be fast. Her nearly black hair was well-coifed and her steady brown eyes were trustworthy.

As they rode, they had much to remember and talk about besides the education at Oberlin. While Harvey had convinced Emeline that she should marry a minister because he was going to be one, their future had been sharply changed by the year just finished.

In 1836, Marcus Whitman, a physician, and Henry Spalding, a minister, had gone with their wives to the "far West" to open a Mission under their sponsors, the Boston-based American Board for Foreign Missions established by the Congregationalists and Presbyterians. Within a few years, it became a Congregational board, better known as "The American Board." The reports sent to the constituents in the East glowed with information, and "more missionaries needed" was the cry. Then, in 1838, the students learned that four couples were being sent west to join the Whitman mission. This looked like a more challenging field than foreign missions across the ocean, and it was certainly more exciting than home missions in the states near Oberlin.

As news came in, the young men at Oberlin held intense meetings to discuss how their own lives might be affected in the future. For the young women—and nearly one-third of the student body was women—the question became two-fold: whether to teach or "to spread the gospel among the heathen." Perhaps Harvey's persuasive answer to Emeline was, "Do both. When you marry me you can teach *and* spread the gospel."

Discussions continued with intensity, as evidenced by one student's report in the *Student Monthly*:

> Last evening, meeting of the Missionary Society. Report on Indians beyond the Rocky Mountains. The facts of the Report were new, and all of thrilling interest.... The region on the whole is very inviting as a missionary field. If I were now ready, I should be glad to go. Perhaps, however, I ought to go where there is more to endure.[1]

---

1   Hornell, Rev. George T.

While it was unsigned, it does show the depth of thought expressed and the seriousness of their decisions.

There was another closer influence, and that was Rev. Charles Finney, forty years of age and a popular evangelist, who was Professor of Theology at Oberlin at this time. Both Harvey Clark and John Griffin had been among Finney's thirty-five students. Finney had earlier been pastor of the Antwerp (New York) Congregational Church, which Harvey and Emeline had attended. Dr. Finney made it clear how dear the mission was to his heart.

John Griffin, upon graduating in the Theology Department in 1838, wrote to the American Board, feeling sure they would send him to join Dr. Whitman. The reply to his application was a "No. There is no money now available." So, what was he to do?

Dr. Finney's answer, in his deep resonant voice, fanned the flame of missionary fever in his students. As Delaven Leonard wrote:

> Mr. Finney laid down the somewhat ultra and startling dictum that "nobody was fit to be a missionary who was not willing with but an ear of corn in his pocket to start for the Rocky Mountains."[2]

On this advice, John Griffin wrote to his Congregational Church in Litchfield, Connecticut, for money to outfit his trip and pay for his living. The church responded by promising its support, and he was able to buy the essential materials he needed.

An older man, also fired by Finney's exhortations, was Asahel Munger, a colonist who had come to the Oberlin community in 1833 and was a member of the Congregational Church. Asahel and his wife said they would join Griffin, and applied to the local church for support. The church records state that they "cannot feel justified in recommending to Br and Sister Munger to embark on this proposed expedition."[3] The church leaders felt Mr. Munger's

---

2   Leonard, Delavan, *The Story of Oberlin,* chapter on "Oberlin's Contributions to Missions," Oberlin College Library. The American Board felt the Oberlin students seeking missionary service were too liberal to represent the Board, and chose Easterners. Being rejected, the Oberlinites had to ask friends, family or their local churches to finance and outfit them, and were called "Independent" missionaries.

3   Fletcher, Robert Samuel.

age and lack of mental stability would make him unable to face the hardships he would encounter. The Mungers were determined, however, and went without the church's blessing or help. Using their own savings, they joined John Griffin and turned toward Independence, Missouri.

One of Emeline's favorite possessions was her autograph album, which she carried with her. She had begun it in 1834 while in Gouverneur, New York, and some of the signatures were from Antwerp. But the most interesting at this time were the messages of love from friends at the Oberlin Institute when they learned she planned to go with Harvey Clark to the "Far West."

One of the messages mentioned the "Mercy seat on heathen shores." Another said, "I rejoice, my dear Miss Cadwell, that the name [missionary] is to apply to yourself."

And a third, less brief, but meaningful:

> Happy indeed should we be to have your Society longer but we can be but far happier to have you go and tell the dying heathen of Christ.... I trust you may have the pleasure of welcoming to heathen shores many from this beloved institute. Our friends here we hope will scatter up and down the earth.
>
> O.C. Aug. 27, 1837[4]

Harvey and Emeline arrived at Independence, excited and anxious to see their friend, John Griffin. But how unexciting everything looked after all they had heard. There were no wagon trains, only the stores one might find in a frontier town, and hangers-on loafing about. Their disappointment was keen when they learned that the American Fur Brigade had left in April of that year, and the Griffin and Munger parties with it. They were told it was too dangerous to travel alone on the chance that they might catch up with the caravan. In fact, they probably could not even find them at the rate they traveled. The uppermost question was what to do for the months ahead until the next year's brigade would travel.

First, they were married, as they had planned to do on arrival at Independence. Then, a minister who befriended them suggested spending the winter in Quincy, Illinois, just across the Mississippi from St. Louis. It was a thriving town and had had only itinerant preachers since Mr. Turner's depar-

---

4   Pacific University Library.

ture. This must have been the Lord's leading. Harvey and Emeline Clark turned the horse-drawn wagon east to this unexpected venture.

QUINCY, ILLINOIS 1839-40

Quincy was all the Clarks could have hoped for. Mr. Turner, ministering from 1830 to 1838, had organized a Presbyterian Church in 1830, which became Congregational—Clark's denomination—in 1833.

There was a clapboard building, crudely constructed and therefore called "The Lord's Barn" or "God's Barn."[5] Not very complimentary, to be sure, but there was a membership of 242 people, who welcomed Mr. Clark as an interim minister.[6] In addition, there was a ten-acre campground for protracted meetings, an important part of the ministry at that time.

The Clarks "settled in," and Harvey was an enthusiastic and sincere preacher. One of his major themes was the need for missions in the distant West. Regular services were held on Sundays. Seasonally, there were protracted meetings for "soul searching", a campground community experience that might last a week or more, with emphasis on saving the unchurched who might attend.

There were many, no doubt, who listened to the Clark message and felt the influence of their young minister, but just three who thought seriously of a western mission and did something about it.

One, Alvin T. Smith, was a bachelor from Connecticut who had come to Fairfield (now Mendon), Illinois, in May 1838, where his brother was a farmer. Mr. Smith was a farmer also, a tall, solidly built, muscular man. He was also a very religious man, and joined the Quincy church in September 1838. He was meticulous in keeping a day-by-day account of all he did over the years. His diary consisted of papers that he folded in 4-1/2 by 5-1/2 inch folios, and sewed together to make pocket-sized booklets. It is these notes that give us details today of the Quincy days and trail data that followed, as a record of the Clark party's travels in the West.

The second and third were P.B. Littlejohn, a lay preacher, and his wife Adelaide. They were regular attendants at Mr. Clark's meetings. Adelaide Saddler Littlejohn was a friend of Narcissa Prentiss Whitman, and had

---

5   *The Herald Whig.*
6   *History of Quincy (Ill.) and Adams County.*

applied to the American Board for work in a foreign mission field, but being single she was not acceptable. She and P.B. Littlejohn were married and applied for service, but still there was no money in the American Board budget.[7] They had come as close to Independence as Quincy, and there they stopped. Naturally, they saw opportunity in Harvey Clark's stimulating sermons, as he urged those interested to join him as independent missionaries in the foreign land to the west.

The winter passed and enthusiasm increased. By February 1840, most of Smith's and the Littlejohns' time was spent at Clark's meetings. Alvin Smith's diary shows his growing commitment:

> Feb 12th talked some about going over the rocky mountains
> Feb 13th ditto and prayed about it
> Feb 14th did the same & concluded to go
> Feb 17th went to collect means to go over the Mt
> Feb 24th went to fairfield to solicit funds for my outfit

From then on, it was a matter of getting cloth for his new shirts, which the Fairfield church ladies would make for him, getting boards for his wagon bed and a plow to take west.

> Mar 9th staid in Quincy & had an interview with Miss Abigail Raymond concerning going with me
> Mar 24th make some preparation for the journey & get a license to get married to Miss Abigail Raymond

Smith's next days were spent taking Mrs. Littlejohn to Quincy or to Columbus, dividing land with his brother, Alfred, and on

> Mar 19th tended to some packing of my things in Fairfield and was married in the evening at Mr. Kirby's & staid all night

Abigail Smith was number four in the party with the Clarks. When Abigail reported to her church, the officers bade her godspeed:

Columbus Adams Co. Illinois
March 15, 1840

---

7   Houghton Library.

This certifies that Miss Abigail Raymond is a member of the Presbyterian Church in regular standing, and at her request is dismissed for the purpose of joining a mission to the Indians in the Oregon Territory – And may the Angel of the Covenant encamp round about thee! till thy labors end, and thy rest is perfect in the Church above.

By Order of the Session

J Frederick Collins, Clerk[8]

Alvin Smith did not detail the trip to St. Louis from Quincy. From there they had to follow the river to Independence. It took them several days, staying with people overnight that Smith names. Though the trip was short, Clark's horse "acted bad" and one of Smith's "was sick."

INDEPENDENCE, MISSOURI

Independence buzzed with activity as newcomers milled around, asking questions, debating about supplies, livestock to take and the value of horses versus mules; checking wagons; and securing any information from those who had returned from the West. Too, it was a time to get acquainted with those who planned to make the 1840 trip across the Oregon Trail.

Some planned to go southwest on the Santa Fe Trail; that group assembled at Independence. Those for the Northwest, or Oregon Trail to the Rockies, gathered twelve miles west at Westport, where the American Fur Brigade would form. To be sure, the old Santa Fe and Oregon Trails were one for forty-one miles before they separated.[9]

Among those the Clark party met was Henry Black.[10] He was not going west as a missionary and he was not a real frontiersman. His only reason for

---

8   Danforth Collection of Smith papers, Oregon Historical Society, Portland. The day-by-day account by Alvin T. Smith is also located at the Oregon Historical Society.

9   Wislizenius, P., M.D.

10   Scott, Harvey W., *History of Oregon Country*, vol. 3. The six volumes by Scott, who witnessed the development of the Territory, are valuable in their detail and description of events and people.

making the trip was his curiosity to see what it would be like. This seems to be the only data on him, and he is not mentioned after departure, so he may have chosen the Santa Fe Trail.

Then there was Pleasant M. Armstrong.[11] He had been born in New York State in 1815. He was a Presbyterian, but not a missionary. As a settler, he became active as a member of the American Party at Champoeg, May 2, 1843, and was one of the organizers of the provisional government.

Unfortunately, he was killed in battle with the Rogue (River) Indians in September 1853, before he had time to more than make a beginning.

George Davis was listed as leaving Independence with the Clark party for the trail to Oregon, but there is no additional information about his background, nor did he take part in later events.

Robert Moore was a Pennsylvanian and planned to settle in the Oregon country. He was an active, positive man, prepared to take his place in the new land, as evidenced later in his leadership in forming the provisional government.[12]

The Joel Walker family was going west too. Joel was popular because he could answer anybody's questions. He had already made the trip west and returned some years earlier. Also, he had a brother, Joseph, a professional mountain man who had made regular crossings over the years.[13] Joel Walker claimed that this would be "the first train of emigrants to Oregon." As a non-missionary settler, he was taking a wife and three children to settle in the new land.[14]

Joel Walker was expecting friends with their families any day to go with him as settlers. They had promised Joel they would be there in plenty of time.

The men in the Clark party from Quincy were busy lining up horses and supplies for the trip.

---

11   *Ibid.*

12   *Ibid.*

13   Clarke, S.A. page 449.

14   Walker, Joel P., "Narrative of Adventure," a hand-written manuscript, Bancroft Library, Berkeley, CA. There are two manuscripts in his file. The first lists a wife and three children. The second, apparently written later, lists four children. The fourth child was perhaps the one born after his arrival in Oregon.

Alvin Smith, too, was getting around, and learning a bit as he went. He wrote:

April 8th went to Westport and to the Shawnee Mission
April 9th went to look for mules
      went to hear the Indians sing in the evening

April 10th, Smith returned to Independence. Except for Sunday, the next four days were spent looking for a good buy in mules. This was an important investment. One could not afford to start such a long, hard trip without the best horses and mules available. This meant repeated trips, haggling on prices, picking healthy (not old) horses and mules that would be strong.

Sunday was a day of prayer and preaching under Mr. Clark. But on April 16th, Smith was back at Westport to trade his horses, and on the 18th, "sold and delivered one of my horses and went to Westport and back to Independence." On the 10th, he traded a horse of a Mr. Smart for a span of mules.

With the animals under control, the next several days saw Mr. Smith "repairing my wagon and helpt about shoeing the mules." Unhappily, Clark and Littlejohn kept no records of what they were doing.

The women had their work to do as well. They busied themselves collecting and packing the supplies in quantity for the long trip ahead of them. Eggs were packed in barrels of corn meal to prevent breakage. The corn meal, too, would be used for cooking on the road. Food stuffs that would not spoil—such items as potatoes, rice, preserves, dried fruits and pickles—had to be securely packed. Coffee and tea were preferable to water unless there was clean stream water with no bugs. It was a consuming job.

Chapter 2
The Oregon Trail: April 1840

The goods were loaded in the three wagons of the Clark party, and with horses, mules and seventeen cows, the three families set out for Westport to meet the American Fur Brigade under the leadership of Capt. Andrew Drips. The date was April 29, 1840, and Quincy seemed far away.

Capt. Drips had been leading brigades to the Green River Rendezvous (in present-day Wyoming) for enough years to know how many days must be allowed for the journey. His responsibility was to be at the rendezvous *on time* for the week of bartering and buying furs to take east.

He explained the rules of travel on which he insisted. Those traveling with his brigade must keep up with the pace he set. If they lagged behind, it was up to them to defend themselves; he would not be responsible. The emigrant group did not relish being left, and was determined to keep up the pace.

The second rule was that there would be no Sunday layovers for rest and spiritual matters. There would be seven days of travel every week until they reached the rendezvous, except when they arrived at designated forts, where layovers and repairs would be made.

His brigade was one of a number of very small parties that went to the Northwest in 1836, '38, '39 and '40. In those years, the American Fur Company, making one trip West to the rendezvous each spring, was willing to take anyone who wanted security in travel. While there was no special cost, the fellow travelers were expected to take their turns on guard duty and share in protecting the brigade if needed. After the rendezvous, the travelers had to find their own guides to the Oregon Country.

Capt. Drips knew that this rendezvous might very well be his last, for the fur-bearing animals were no longer plentiful and he had traveled for the American Fur Company since 1831. This period also marked the end of

11

such informal travel arrangements. By the mid-1840s when the big migrations came, the strong farmers' wagons and light spring wagons, drawn by mules or horses, were replaced by Conestoga wagons drawn by oxen. This caused difficulties when crossing hills and mountain passes because the large, unwieldy Conestogas had to be held back by ropes drawn around trees, and sheer, brute strength was needed to keep the wagons from running down the oxen.

The next day, April 29, the brigade moved out. The fur company led the way with thirty two-wheeled carts, each drawn by two mules. These were followed by pack mules loaded with goods for trade with the trappers and Indians.[1] Forty men traveled with Capt. Drips. Some were scouts, some were hunters and others were drivers. Following the brigade were the ten emigrants—six independent missionaries and four laymen, Henry Black, Pleasant Armstrong, George Davis and Robert Moore. The Joel Walkers had not arrived and the brigade would wait for no one.

They covered only four miles and camped.

There were no definite roads. Since it was a large expanse of prairie, the early wagon trails crisscrossed earlier wagon ruts. The prairie allowed faster travel than there would be when the hill country was reached. Too, the prairie was relatively safer than traveling through timber. Later, wagon trains would be so large that deep ruts could not be avoided. They were so deep that even a century later, many of those ruts were still visible.[2]

At the end of the day's trip, April 30, Mr. Smith noted:

> traveled 12 miles & camped at Sapalin grove
> May 1 traveled 25 miles camped at Elm grove traveled on the pararie [sic] all day
> met a company of caw Indians

At this point, forty-one miles of trail had been covered, and the Oregon-bound brigade turned northwest toward the mountains.

Alvin Smith mentioned seeing a company of Caw Indians. Later, he reported crossing the "Caw or Kansas River," so apparently the band was

---

1   Bancroft Library.
2   Paden, Irene. Three members of the Paden party followed the Oregon Trail west from Independence, locating rest stops and places passed by the emigrants, finding wagon tracks and information on Indians of that early period.

Kanza Indians. The Indians were much different from the ones Smith had visited in Westport under American missionaries.

We are told that the Indian women "wore leather over-shirts and loose drawers." The Kanza men shaved their heads, leaving a brush of hair on top of the head, from forehead to neck. Into this hair they fastened feathers for decoration. They ringed their eyes with vermilion paint and wore only a loin cloth, except for an occasional blanket if needed.[3]

The emigrants began to learn about enmities among the Indians, as well as the fact that different tribes had their own characteristics. For instance, the Shawnee and the Kanza were enemies. The Kanza Indians were always alert to danger if Shawnees approached. The emigrants perceived the Sioux as very arrogant; the Sioux, Crow and Cheyenne Indians further west were seen as friendly or hostile, depending on how the chieftain reacted.[4]

But there was one thing all Indians they met seemed to have in common: curiosity. They would travel near the group, often overstaying their welcome, just to see what the emigrants were doing.

Each day saw new miles covered—twenty miles, twelve miles, fifteen miles. And each night the campground differed—one night in a mulberry grove after a storm, or on a rocky hill, another time "camped on a stony creek bottom" after a good day's travel.

On May 5th, having traveled fifty-eight miles from Westport, they arrived at "and crossed the Caw or Kansas River in a canoe had the wagons halled [sic] over by hand by the company."[5]

At such crossings, the animals had to swim, which filled the air with bellowing and braying over the shouting of riders on horses to keep them moving. If the water was too deep, wheels were removed and the wagons were floated across by men on horseback. This was not necessary at the Kansas, according to Smith's report.

The day after the crossing, Joel Walker and his family in three wagons overtook the brigade. Joel had waited hopefully for some of his forty people who had promised to go west with him as settlers. To his disappointment, not one had shown up. He knew he could wait no longer for his friends; he must hurry to catch the brigade before it reached dangerous country.[6]

---

3   *Ibid.*
4   *Ibid.*
5   Oregon Historical Society.
6   Bancroft Library.

Two days after crossing the Kansas River, the brigade came to "the perpendicular bank of the Red Vermilion" which was the "boundary between the Pottowatomes and the Pawnees."[7] The brigade thought the Pawnees were unpredictable and had to be watched.

Guard duty immediately became necessary, and each man served the time assigned to him until relieved by the next guard. Smith does not mention this in his diary, but it was understood that all able-bodied men took their share of guard duty. It was believed that the Pawnees were silent in their stalking and usually after horses, so night watch was seen as imperative.

Each day, Alvin Smith jotted down a line or two—the trail was good or it was bad. The days were windy or dry. There were creeks to cross: "spring bluff creek, frog hole creek," and there were "bur oak barrens" after crossing the "little blue river" on May 13th.

The freshness of the trip had worn off. Now it was dry and dusty, as illustrated in the Smith report:

May 14th traveled 20 miles through pararie & no water between camps
    camped on big blue river

May 15th traveled 20 miles most of the way on the blue bottom camped on
    the bottom right by the creek bank

May 16th Traveled 22 miles along by the creek camped on the creek broke
    my wagon tongue and bounds 2 miles from the encampment tied it up
    & went to camp & went to work & put in a new pair of bounds & got
    done at 1 o'clock at night

May 17th Sabbath traveled 4 miles along the big blue camped on the water
    of it in a little hollow

As had become usual, the Sabbath was not a day of rest, but of travel, and it would be evening before a religious session could be held with Clark as leader.

On May 18th, the brigade approached the Platte River with its sand hills and dunes. Smith noted, "Two men came up to camp at noon that had been robbed by the Pawnees." This reinforced the brigade's beliefs about the Pawnees.

---

7   Paden, Irene.

14

Now they traveled along the south bank of the Platte and saw "flocks of antelope." On May 23, they saw something that brought home to them the hazards of this trip.

> May 23rd   traveled 26 miles on the river bottom passed 2 graves a white
> man & Indians I saw herds of buffalo company killed we got some of it
> & cooked it with buffalo maneure [*sic*]

By this time, wood for cooking had disappeared. But there was plenty of dried buffalo manure available, and it made a good hot fire for cooking.

Every day there seemed to be more buffalo. One day, Smith estimated 1,000, and another day, 3,000 buffalo. But the brigade hunters did not kill for fun, only for each day's food.

One night, ten "shian" [Cheyenne] Indians were at camp. There was also word that Jim Bridger was coming. He was a well-known mountain man and trapper, well-acquainted with Capt. Drips and his men. Bridger had not appeared on May 28th when the brigade "watered over the north fork" of the Platte.

On the 29th, Jim Bridger arrived at camp. The hunters killed three buffalo, so there was fresh meat to enhance the limited diet, as well as good company with Bridger and his stories at this camp. Smith reckoned they had covered 628 miles since leaving Westport, arriving in present-day Nebraska, and for the first time mentions something that reminded him of home:

> May 30th traveled 28 miles saw in the bottom what I should call in the salt
> meadows in Connecticut goose grass by smells & looks saw lots of
> buffalo company killed only 1 camped by the river in sight of the rock
> castle so called & in sight of the chimney so called

> May 31st Sabbath traveled 27 miles camped between the chimney & the
> river

On the morning of June 1st, they went to "view Chimney Rock but I found it to be a point [of] clay 200 feet high." June 4th, the brigade "camped by the laramas fork [Laramie] by the fort of the same name close by 30 lodges of the Shian Indians."

The next four days, June 8-11, were dismal and exhausting. The country was "rough and poor" day after day. Smith called it "broken country." They were in sight of the "black hills with snow on them."

15

On June 12th, the monotony was broken by something worse. They now had to cross the north fork of the Platte River. There was no shade, the river was wide and shallow, the water was dirty and there was a bed of quicksand to avoid. It was considered a bad fork and took careful planning.[8]

Alvin Smith's diary at this point is quite detailed:

> June 12th   traveled 3 miles & came to the crossing & camped company made a boat of willows & buffalo hides & made preparations for crossing & had a verry [sic] heavy shower & hail & wind

> June 13th   crossed our things over the river in the boat & floated the wagon beds over & put our wagons together & went to get the mules to hall it to the goods & a heavy shower of wind & hail came up which drove my wagon into the river & upset the wagon. The body came off & floated down about 20 rods & lodged the running the same & lost the rocker king bolt cupling bolt & hammer we halled it out & made a rocker of cotton wood & loaded up & traveled 28 miles & camped by the river which took til after sundown

> June 14th   Sabath traveled 15 miles & camped for the last time by the platt river & onloaded [sic] the things & dried them by the fire & help of the sun & packed them up again the hunters killed 8 buffalo & plenty of snow in sight of our camp

While Alvin Smith was experiencing near catastrophe, Joel Walker reported no mishaps, saying, "We got along without trouble, and crossed the North Platte in Buffalo Skin Boats."[9]

After the Platte crossing, there were four days of "poor, sandy soil." The only excitement was that the hunters killed "4 buffalo and 2 grisley bears." But on June 17th, the party came to "sweet water at Independent rock." This interested Alvin Smith, and he "went on to it & paced it 620 paces long." The next day, they passed "the gape [sic] in the rock where the sweet water passed through the rocks each side perpendicular 150 feet high."[10]

The country continued to be poor, and the "traveur" to Smith's "forward bounds" broke and had to be repaired. One day they did not travel, and

---

8   *Ibid.*
9   Bancroft Library.
10   Oregon Historical Society.

Smith went out with the hunters "and brought in some meat to dry." They were nearing the rendezvous, and as the brigade passed a Snake village the Indians followed and camped with them.

> June 25th passed the divide between the water of the Missourie [*sic*] & Colorado. The Indians all around us.

The next day they reached the headwaters of the Colorado, and on Sunday, June 28th, the ice was one-half inch thick. On June 29, they reached the Green River Rendezvous, now Wyoming, which was as far as the American Fur Brigade would go. They had covered 1,284 miles, according to Smith's figuring.

All around were trappers with furs to sell and Indians who wanted to trade and barter. A good many of the mountain men had brought their Indian wives and children. There were fewer furs than in prior years, and Capt. Drips was right in calling this the last and smallest of the rendezvous. A part of the early West was dying. But even this last rendezvous was lively, with games, races and feats of prowess. The valley where the rendezvous was held was large and clear. It offered adequate space for wagons, tents and wigwams, and forage for the horses and cattle which had been strong enough to survive the trip.

The next five days in camp were a restful change, in spite of the noise of so many voices, yet Alvin Smith wrote that he "staid in camp & was verry sick" on the 2nd of July. The next day, Smith left the company, traveled five miles, crossed the river and made his camp, wrote to his brother and rested.

Joel Walker's report, written later, was more detailed:

> At the Independence Rock, near the mouth of the Sweetwater, we met a large company of Snake Indians, and travelled with them, sometime two weeks. From this point we crossed the Rocky Mountains to the head waters of the Green River and spent the 4th of July on that river.[11]

On July 5, under the guidance of Bill Craig, one of the men under Joel Walker's brother, the small Clark party and the Walkers began the next part of their journey to Fort Hall, now Idaho. The trip was not easy. The country

---

11   Bancroft Library.

was rough in sections, so in one day only 20 miles might be covered, and on another, only 11 to 14 miles. It was a relief whenever a good trail appeared.

Arrival at Soda Springs, now Idaho, at noon created some variety, but they did not linger. On the night of July 18th, they camped at the headwaters of the Columbia River.

On July 20, the party arrived at Fort Hall, ending a 22-mile day. Here, the party was told wagons could not make the last stage of the trip and would have to be left behind. Clark and Smith met Joe Meek, a mountain man, his brother-in-law, Robert Newell, and a friend named Ermatinger. All of them emphasized how the going would be too rough, and wagons simply could not make it.

Being convinced by their arguments, Smith wrote:

> July 21st dispose of my wagon conditionally to have & pack horse loads 1880 lbs of goods delivered to walla walla for the wagon to have it back if I wish for the same which amounts to 80 dollars I've packed a part of my goods

> July 22nd finished packing the goods packed up our horse & traveled 10 miles & camped by the river called portnuff [Portneuf, Idaho]

The Clark and Littlejohn wagons were disposed of in the same way. The cattle, now worn out and footsore, were left at Fort Hall, to be replaced by Mexican stock that would be delivered when they arrived at a destination.

Indians followed them and they camped on July 24 on what Smith called "stolen horse creek." It may be that the party gave the camp its name after their experience, for that night "2 Indians traveling with us stole my riding horse & 1 of Mr. Walker's & hid them in the willows but got them in the morning." Both Smith and Walker were relieved to get their horses.

A change of diet was a joy when, on July 29, the party arrived at the Salmon Falls where it joins the Snake River. They found a different type of Indians. They were friendly and talkative, and they were eager to sell their salmon and the little cakes they made of lizards, crickets and grasshoppers. They were using rabbit skins as covering, and they bartered for clothing, and even more eagerly for fish hooks. Their living seemed simple to the party. For sustenance, they appeared to primarily fish for salmon in the river, for which steel fish hooks were helpful.[12]

---

12   Paden, Irene.

Smith noted that July 30 was the first day they had not been in sight of snow. But he was even more cheered when he was able to write:

> August 2nd Sabath did not travel today but for the first whole sabath since we started that we lay by the rest of the company went on we had a prayer meeting & Bible class

> August 4th traveled 12 miles & camped opposite fort Boise went to the fort and got some milk to drink staid in camp the rest of the day

> August 5th stopped to noon by a creek at the hot springs & cooked a part of our salmon in the hot spring

> August 8th camped at the lone tree & experienced a heavy thunder shower of rain

The lone pine tree was a beautiful, well-proportioned tree that stood like a sentinel in an open meadow. It had become a landmark, which emigrants looked forward to reaching for relaxation and a comfortable camp. (It is sad to report that a few years later, after the big migrations, the lone tree was no longer there. It had been cut down and used by the travelers as they passed.)

The land began to look better. There were blue hills and rich, fertile bottom land as they "camped on the grand round [Grande Ronde]." The Clark party of six was now dependent on one another, since Walker and his party had taken a more southerly route in hopes of finding a quicker way to Oregon.

On August 12th, they met Indians who came to their camp before breakfast. One of the visitors was engaged to act as their guide and pilot. One more mountain stood in front of them as they camped in the pines at its base. The next day they understood why they had been advised not to take their wagons.

> August 13th traveled 38 miles over the blue hills some of the way a fine pine country camped in pine hollow by cold river after descending a mountain an hour and a half long

> August 14th rose a mountain an hour & a halfs travel long came through some fine timber & a rough country traveled 35 miles & arrived at Doctor Whitmans

They had been on the road since April 30th, some three and a half months. They had traveled, according to Smith's reckoning, 2,111 miles from Westport to the Whitman Mission. It must have been good to see fellow Americans, since at that time there were fewer than 15 Americans within a day's ride the Mission, near what is now Walla Walla. Adelaide Littlejohn in particular, must have anticipated a joyful reunion with her friend, Narcissa Whitman.

The Whitmans welcomed the weary travelers. They were eager for fellow ministers in the West. They saw it as a large expanse of territory, with room for all ministers, regardless of whether they were independent or American Board members.

And what of the Walker party, which left the Clarks to take another route? Joel Walker's narrative completes his part of this story:

> Clark and myself with our families went through the mountains to a fork of the Lewis River, and turned Southwest to Fort Hall. The wagons got there ten days afterward. We then arranged to pack to Oregon. We were well treated at Fort Hall by the Hudsons Bay Company. From here we travelled down Snake River to Fort Boise, and from there without any trouble, westward, to Fort Vancouver. This party formed the

First Train of Emigrants to Oregon

> From Vancouver I proceeded across the Columbia and [southward] up the Willamette valley to a place near the present location of Salem, the capitol of Oregon, and remained there until 1841....

> My daughter Louisa was born in Oregon January 14th, 1841, the first white child born in Oregon of American parents.

Later in 1841, the Walkers moved south to California and settled near Sacramento.[13]

---

13   Walker, Joel, Bancroft Library.

Chapter 3
The Whitman Mission

The new arrivals very shortly became aware of personal restraint, if not antagonism, toward them—not by the Whitmans, but by the other missionary couples.

To understand this lack of welcome from Whitman's fellow missionaries, we must understand the background of Whitman's venture in the context of representing the American Board, the Congregational Presbyterian Foreign Missionary Society in Boston, which had sent the Whitmans and Spaldings west to found their mission among the Indians.

In taking on the cause of foreign missions in the far West, the American Board had tried to anticipate what situations might be expected by sending Dr. Marcus Whitman, a Congregationalist from Rushville, New York, and a well-educated medical man, to survey the land in 1834 and decide where missions might be placed among the Indians.

Arriving at Fort Vancouver, Whitman was warmly received by Dr. John McLoughlin, head factor of the Hudson's Bay Company. A large middle-aged man, he had a dignified bearing and a head of white hair, which added to his dignity and earned him the name, "The White-Headed Eagle." He was clearly in command, and yet was benevolent in his helpfulness.

The two men found they had much in common as both were physicians. McLoughlin was also educated in law, and having been at Fort Vancouver since 1824, knew his country and the Indians well. He was glad to share his knowledge and advise Whitman on prospects for an Indian mission.

Whitman, having absorbed the facts he needed, renewed his travel east to Fort Walla Walla, looked over the land and went back to Boston with his report.

It was decided that the first missionaries were to go west with the Fur Traders in 1836. Two men would be sent, who were to marry after being commissioned for service and just before departure. Dr. Whitman had chosen Narcissa Prentiss, a talented musician with a beautiful singing voice, who would make an excellent helpmate. She was from Plattsville, New York.

A second couple was harder to choose. Several men were spoken to, but the west did not appeal to them. The final choice was Rev. Henry Spalding, a man from Narcissa's home town. Unfortunately, he had earlier been infatuated with Narcissa, but she had rejected his overtures. This rankled Spalding and eventually caused problems; however, he accepted the American Board's offer and found a wife to accompany him.

With them also went William H. Gray, a mechanic, who would spend the rest of his life in the Oregon Territory.

In those days, there was no question in the minds of American Board members as to whether or not the missionaries could stand up to the rigors of this new life. When traveling west, for example, the women would ride sidesaddle, while the goods were carried in wagons. It was an untried venture, and few guidelines were available. Fortunately, the missionaries were young and healthy.

The American Board did provide a meager allowance of money before they started out, but the missionaries were warned that they must become self-supporting as soon as possible. They were given no other knowledge of the Indian languages or what crops could be raised. This left them at a distinct disadvantage.

It was understood that Dr. Whitman was to head the mission project. But, Spalding eyed Narcissa with dislike and was unhappy to be under another man's leadership—especially the husband of this woman who had spurned his affection.

They arrived at Fort Vancouver without incident. McLoughlin welcomed the two women, hoping they could be friends with his wife and daughter. McLoughlin tried to persuade Whitman to go south to the Willamette Valley where Jason Lee had located, but Whitman was determined to go east to Fort Walla Walla. At this time, Narcissa sent a letter to her mother:

> The Nez Perces are exceedingly anxious for the location [in their territory]. Make many promises to work and listen to instruction. They do not like to have us stop with the Cayouses [the Cayuse tribe]. Say they do not have difficulty with the white man as the Cayouses do & that we shall find it so.[1]

She went on to say that Dr. Whitman's decision was to locate on the Walla Walla River, 25 miles east of Fort Walla Walla, "the country of the Cayouses, who speak the same language as the Nez Perces." Whitman called his site "Waiilatpu." He sent Spalding 10 miles east to locate on the north side of the Snake River, to a place called Lapwai. There they set about preaching and teaching the Indians.

Whitman was versatile and industrious, and by 1839 had a mill on his stream and was raising a field of wheat. But Whitman felt the Indians were not helpful and were not willing to learn. He reported that they rode their horses through his wheat and were angry when he reprimanded them.

Mrs. Whitman found it most trying when the Indians would walk into her home uninvited and watch to see how the Whitmans lived. When the doors were closed to give the Whitmans a measure of privacy, the Indians stood outside looking in the window.

In spite of all this, Whitman was enthusiastic about the future of his mission, and wrote to the American Board in Boston for recruits.

In 1838, the Board responded by sending three mission couples: Rev. Elkinah and Mary Walker, Rev. Cushing and Myra Eells, and Rev. Asa B. Smith and his young wife. They also sent a layman, Cornelius Rogers. They traveled west with the American Fur Company, as the Whitmans and Spaldings had done. And, as in 1836, the women rode sidesaddle all the way, except as they chose to walk or ride in the wagon when there was room. At night, the three couples slept in one large tent, with curtains to separate them. Even curtained privacy was limited, as the young Mrs. Smith could be heard crying, and the whispering of some couples was distracting to the others. Since they were all so recently wed and not too long acquainted with each other, it was a trying and difficult journey.

If Capt. Drips, the brigade leader, was distressed by the missionaries, it was because he knew that his men were being critically judged according to Eastern standards. Neither could the missionaries accept the mountain men who had married Indian women and had children together.

Bernard de Voto, in his book, *Across the Wide Missouri*, described this mission group as a "peripatetic slugging match for heavenly favor." In defense of the missionary couples, we must accept the fact that each minister had set opinions, not necessarily agreeing with his co-workers, and religion was a very serious business. No wonder there was not perpetual harmony among one another in the face of the new world they were entering.

---

1   Houghton Library.

So, with the new arrivals, Mrs. Whitman was overjoyed to "have the society of our brethern and sisters who eat at our table and expect to spend the winter here."[2]

That fall, Walker and Eells went exploring and located a mission at Tshim-a-kain, a site just north of the Spokane River and 30 miles south of the present city of Spokane. They were the furthest removed from the Whitman Mission. In the spring, Rev. A. B. Smith and his wife Sara located a mission at Kamiah on the Clearwater, 70 miles above the present city of Lewiston, Idaho. Sara Smith, young and inexperienced, had wept a good deal of the way west. Now at Kamiah, she felt she was at the end of the world, with no ability to adjust to this new life. Fortunately, she had a patient and understanding husband.

Again, the American Board was sending messages urging the missionaries to achieve a position of self-support and relieve the pressure for money from the East—and this after only two years, at most, of settling in a strange land. McLoughlin had furnished seeds and foodstuffs, and given animals with the proviso that an equal amount would be returned to him when it was possible to do so. This gesture was most appreciated by the newcomers.

A second edict of the American Board was that if any independent missionaries should appear at these sponsored missions, they were not to receive any encouragement. In fact, they would not be acceptable. Independent missionaries could be anybody who came without American Board sanction.

At first, there had been great joy at the arrival of the three new missionary couples and meetings were held regularly at Waiilatpu, under Whitman's leadership, for discussion of the work at the four mission stations. Now, in 1839, the sessions began to take on tones of grumbling and distrust of each other's methods of service. Even before they had learned to communicate with each other, they were fearful of any threatening independents who might come.

And come they did in 1839 in the form of Rev. John Griffin and a very capable wife he had met in Independence, and Asahel Munger and wife from Oberlin. With them was Dr. William Geiger, a physician and friend of Dr. Whitman's, and a Mr. Johnson who did not stay long.

The arrival of the Griffins and Mungers presented a dilemma. What to do with them? They had been told not to befriend them, but send them on their way. In a conference, the mission group discovered they did not agree

---

2 *Ibid.*

with each other. But the final decision was to discourage the independents and send Griffin and Munger as far from their territory as possible.

Griffin stayed at the Whitmans' mission only a short time, then went with his wife to Fort Vancouver where he acted as a chaplain. While McLoughlin was a Catholic, he welcomed ministers equally, feeling that the country needed religion and ethics, whatever the religious persuasion.

Dr. Whitman found that Asahel Munger was a knowledgeable carpenter, and hired him at Waiilatpu to complete his new house. Munger was paid eight dollars a month plus family supplies. He further proved his usefulness by making furniture for the Whitmans—a spinning wheel and folding blinds for the windows.

The Whitmans had made one room in the new house available to the Indians. They could come into only this room, and church services were held in the Indian room. When the Indians asked why they were barred from the rest of the family house, Mrs. Whitman told them it was because she thought they were dirty and had lice.

Now and then, Griffin, a most unhappy man, would come by. He was sure he was better educated than the ministers sent by the Board, but he did not have the first idea of how to go about founding a mission or where it should be located. At least Dr. Whitman showed him kindness and made Griffin and his wife welcome whenever they came by.

Wisely, Dr. Whitman had built a grist mill, finding it cheaper to grind his own wheat. He saw it, too, as a necessity since the Whitman Mission became the first stop for anyone crossing the Oregon Trail to Fort Walla Walla and west. But Spalding was a jealous man and envious of Whitman's achievements, and found in Griffin a sympathetic ear. This did not help maintain peace in the four mission stations, and they began writing their grievances to the American Board. The letters took so long to send and get replies, however, that individual problems might be solved before the answers arrived.

Mrs. Whitman, writing to her father on October 10, 1840, expressed her grief and worry about Henry Spalding:

> The man who came with us is one who ought never to have come. My dear husband has suffered more from him in consequence of his wicked jealousy and his great pique toward me, than can be known in this world. But he suffers not alone. The whole mission suffers which is most to be deplored.[3]

---

3   *Ibid.*

It was into this atmosphere of controversy and antagonism that the Clarks, Smiths and Littlejohns arrived—three independent missionary couples to swell the problems of the American Board missionaries. While the Whitmans welcomed them at Waiilatpu, Mr. Spalding wrote to Rev. David Greene in Boston about these self-supporting missionaries:

> Mr. and Mrs. Griffin who left this March to explore the Snake Country were shut up in the Mts several weeks by impossible snow. Did not reach [the] Snake Fork till the last of May & after spending a few weeks in exploring returned to Waiilatpu without selecting a location. Has since traveled in a southwest direction.

The next paragraph of the Spalding letter reported on the arrival of the Clark party:

> Last month Revd Clark and Messrs Smith and Littlejohn arrived at Waiilatpu to join Messrs Griffin & Munger. Their destination I know not. I told Mr. G. on his return from the Snake Country that though I had great confidence in his judgment I would not nevertheless hesitate to take my family & effects, were I at liberty to direct my effort, to the Snake tribe and go directly to the field he has abandoned and pronounced uninhabitable.

The following paragraph expresses Spalding's philosophy as a missionary. Perhaps it represented that of all the Board missionaries:

> A man coming to the country with the purpose of benefitting its miserable inhabitants must in the first place (taking it for granted that it is settled as to the last request of our risen Lord) give himself, heart and Body, to a given tribe.... He is going to a tribe to teach them & die with them.... If they [the Indians] have lived & do die in that country I can....[4]

---

4   Spalding, letter to Greene in Boston about his philosophy as a missionary. The American Board letters are in the Houghton Library, however, copies of some are in the Oregon Historical Society and/or the three volumes of *Marcus Whitman, Crusader,* by Hurlbert & Hurlbert

Chapter 4
A Year of Decisions: 1841-1842

As the days passed at the Mission, the Clarks and Smiths fitted easily into the life at Waiilatpu. The first day there, Smith went out to hunt for horses.

On the "Sabath [*sic*] Aug 16 Dr. Whitman preached to the Indians," Smith's diary reports, and Smith attended the services after which "we had preaching ourselves."

Alvin Smith helped Munger make a fanning mill to separate chaff from wheat, and Whitman noted how helpful Clark and Smith were in getting in the crops. It was much appreciated and in sharp contrast to Griffin, who had not lifted a hand or offered to help with the harvest the previous year.

Dr. Whitman used Clark on Sundays, as reported by Smith: "Tended meeting and had a communion season [*sic*] and Mr. Clark preached."

Difficulties had arisen between Munger and Griffin and their wives. Alvin Smith took it upon himself to act as mediator, "to try to effect a reconciliation between them for their own good & for the cause of Christ."

By September 8th, the Griffins and Mungers "had partially settled their difficulties." No details are given as to the differences, but they were resolved for a time.

In the meantime, Narcissa Whitman had her problems feeding so many guests. She was still cooking at the fireplace, though stoves had been ordered from the East for both the Whitman and Spalding Missions.

On September 15, the Clark party went on an exploration to see what prospects there might be for beginning their mission to the Indians. Griffin joined them, though the area had not appealed to him on an earlier trip. Clark knew they must find a location for his mission, not too close to the American Board missions and not too far removed from a supply route to Fort Vancouver or Fort Walla Walla. Spalding had been incorrect in his letter to Boston, saying Clark came to join Griffin. That had never been in

Clark's mind. He had only hoped to make the 1839 trip with Griffin and Munger, but there had never been any talk about working together.

The trip lasted two weeks through Cayuse country, and then they were back at Waiilatpu. Rev. Spalding and Rev. A.B. Smith looked upon these independent missionaries with compassion and decided to do something about helping them settle in.

The Spaldings invited the Alvin Smiths to winter with them at Lapwai. The Smiths went on November 9 and stayed into the next year, with an occasional trip to Waiilatpu as necessary. Mr. Smith found much to do. He helped with the corn crop, and fixed up the Spalding grist and saw mills. Seeing that the wool of the sheep was to be used for cloth, he made "a loom and reel for Mrs. Spalding to use in teaching the Indian girls how to weave cloth."

Mr. and Mrs. Clark were invited to winter with the A.B. Smiths at Kamiah, where they stayed until March. The Clarks were helpful, both in a physical and spiritual sense, since the young wife was ill and lonely.

Rev. Asa Smith wrote to his father on February 19, 1841,

> We concluded to remain during the winter. We then invited Rev. Mr. Clark
> and wife, Oberlin missionaries who came out last spring on their own
> responsibility to spend a winter with us. Their company has been a great
> comfort to us. They expect to leave here soon. They are so disappointed that
> they will probably return home.

They did not know Harvey Clark, because he had no intention of turning east. However, he was still uncertain what place he would find for his mission. After the departure of the Clarks, Asa Smith and his wife went home, as Sara's health had worsened.

The Littlejohns remained that winter with the Whitmans. It may be that the three couples in the Clark party served an unexpected purpose as a tonic for the American Board missionaries. Certainly, they gave them new thoughts.

Trouble between the Indians and missionaries had surfaced in 1840, each incident unrelated to the others. "The Nez Perce Indians destroyed the mill at Lapwai, assaulted Spalding with a gun," and reportedly insulted Mrs. Spalding. At the Whitman Mission, the Cayuse Indians "destroyed Dr. Whitman's irrigation ditches, turned their horses into his grain fields, and when reproved had assaulted him with an axe and thrown mud in his face."[1]

Miles Cannon in *Waiilatpu* makes an interesting statement: "Waiilatpu had in the fall of 1840, passed the zenith of its usefulness as a mission, but as a station on the Oregon Trail it yet had work to do."

Alvin Smith was becoming restless as the winter ended, and on February 20, 1841, Littlejohn arrived at the Spalding's. On March 2, Clark arrived. The men discussed their future and went to "view the land up the valley." Nothing appealed to them, and on April 13 they started back to Waiilatpu.

One thing they had learned—that the Indians did not seem to want to be taught by the missionaries. They were also nomadic. They would winter in a location, move on to the hunt, maybe return, and just as likely set up in a fresh spot. Farming did not appear to interest them; to the missionaries, this made them seem unpredictable.

The missionaries had tried to communicate by learning the dialects. Spalding had received a printing press from the Sandwich Islands (as Hawaii was then called), and Cornelius Rogers became the printer, laboriously putting the language down on paper. These efforts were not always successful.

As for the independent missionaries, they had soon discovered it involved much more than Dr. Finney in Oberlin had suggested, when he said all that was needed "was an ear of corn in one's pocket" to found a mission for the Indians in an unknown country.

Dr. Whitman had some sad news to report on March 28, 1841, to the Boston secretary, Rev. David Greene:

> Mr. Munger, who has been with us for some time has become a
> mono-maniac and must be sent home with his family. He has become an
> unsafe man to remain about the mission.

Before he could be returned to the East, he became completely deranged and took his own life.

April 16, 1841, Alvin Smith consulted with Clark about the mission they had come west to establish. When the arrangements to begin a mission to the Indians had been discussed in Quincy, Clark looked on it as a matter to be voted upon by all, insofar as stock and common goods were concerned. Smith understood he had come with Clark to assist in the mission, but not to turn over all he possessed to Mr. Clark's project. There had been

---

1   Cannon, Miles.

no ground rules and no contract. Now, Smith was disturbed by the loose arrangement and the fact that there was no mission.

The meeting lasted two days without resolving the matter to Smith's liking. Finally, a decision was made to go south as Dr. McLoughlin had suggested. Smith went back to Spalding's to pack his things for a move "to the lower country," and on August 25, Smith wrote:

> settled with Mr. Spalding & took an order on Vancouver for 66 & 24/100 dollars & am to have an American heifer & bull hereafter at 50 dollars if the mission is willing.

Spalding had written to the American Board for permission to help Smith, and awaited a reply:

> I have found Mr. Smith & wife very attached to the cause of the missions. They have rendered us great assistance – Mr. Smith in building & farming, Mrs. S. in school. I promised Mr. S. a cow, bull and grain to take with them whenever they find a place to locate.... But on presenting the request at the last meeting, to have permission to pay the cow to Mr. Smith, I was surprised to find all the brethren opposed. Some of the brethren have even censured me because I have...given employment to these self-supporting missionaries.

Spalding finally decided to use his own judgment in supplying the Smiths with animals and grain without waiting for permission.

Harvey Clark had gone to Vancouver to confer with the Hudson's Bay factor, McLoughlin, about settling in the south. He learned that Griffin had settled in the south and Littlejohn was still trying to find a way to go back home. Back at Waiilatpu, Clark preached on August 29, and they left on September 1 for the Willamette Valley.

The trip followed trails through unmarked territory, and several times they lost their sense of direction. Indian guides were not used for this trip. Mr. Smith's diary mentions traveling to "John days river" [sic], and then to the "sand banks between the shoots and dalls." At the Dalles, they found Daniel Lee of the Methodist Mission. Here, they received the news that the warehouse at Fort Walla Walla where they had stored their possessions had burned and everything was destroyed. After a week, and now with Indians in their party, they proceeded to the Wallamut Falls—Oregon City. Smith wrote:

Sept. 15th   traveled 30 miles over mountains and through valleys & camped
     by a little stream in among the tall pines

Sept. 16th   passed mount hood [*sic*] camped on the plane [*sic*] west of it.

Sept. 17th   traveled 10 miles lost 2 of my pack horses hunted some time
     and the Indians found them.

Sept. 18th   traveled 20 miles, was interrupted by the fire lost one of Br.
     Munger's horses camped on a flat by a little rill nearly surrounded by
     fire.
[probably
          a forest fire; no other detail is provided]

The next day, Munger's lost horse was found, and on September 22 the travelers arrived at "the falls of the Wallamut."

The falls were awe-inspiring as they crashed down the solid wall of rock and continued on their course to the sea. There were scattered homes of log, but the location was so advantageous that many travelers stayed at Wallamut Falls instead of going on to the Willamette Valley. The Clark group did not stay long, but hurried on to the East Tualatin Plain to meet Griffin, who now had a log home and preached there on Sundays to any newcomers who came.

Griffin suggested two possible sites south of where he lived, and took Clark and Smith to look them over. Within three days they made their decision—they would settle south of the present site of Hillsboro, but not too near Griffin, who feared competition.

September 28, Alvin Smith wrote, "[We] packt up our animals & went to the place where we expect to locate." The next day, he reported, "We traveled about to look at our place that we intend to claim for the Indians."

They chose to be near a small tribe of Kalapooians that called themselves the Twalatines. There were thirty families in the unit, and they had simple lodges of woven branches laced together. Like all Indians of that period and place, they were nomads.

All Kalapooians in this part of the Oregon Country spoke the same dialect, but they were known by the area names they chose—the Twalatines, the Yamhills and so forth. They were peaceful and seemed to the group to be quite unlike the Cayuse of the Whitman area.

These Indians did not have horses in the early period, until they got them later from settlers. Their meat consisted of deer, which were plentiful, and fish which were abundant in the streams. Camas, a Chinook word for an edible bulb of the lily family that grew wild in the area, and other roots completed their diet. They were short in stature, wore little clothing and slept outdoors unless it was inclement.

It was in this environment that Clark and Smith proposed to open their mission.

Having settled the location for the mission, Alvin Smith set to work making "ax helves." Harvey Clark and Littlejohn "went to the Wallamette" and returned the next day with 12 bushels of potatoes and six of peas. On Sunday they rested and Clark preached.

The Tualatin Plains got their name from the Indians who lived there. But because the settlers spelled it phonetically, it went under several spellings for many years. Dr. Elijah White, agent for Indian Affairs, called it the "Fallatine Plain." Elsewhere, it was spelled "Tuality" or "Twality." Finally, it took today's spelling as the Tualatin Plain, and was further defined as the north, south, east and west plains. These sectors were derived from the areas of prairie bounded by heavy forest growth.

Frances Fuller Victor, writing in 1872, described it as follows:

> Starting at the northern end, on the west side, we should take a look at the so-called Tualatin Plains of Washington County. Immediately upon entering from the heavily timbered Columbia and Wallamet highlands we are struck with the beautiful natural arrangement of the plains and groves. Small prairies, from one to six miles in diameter, are separated by belts of groups of fir and oak intermingled. Growing in more open spaces than the forest affords, and in a soil of green richness, these trees have attained perfection in size and form.[2]

This must represent what the settlers found in 1841, because in early writings the plains were well designated. The Hillsboro area was the East Plain, with the North and South Plains above and below it.

---

2   Victor, Frances Fuller. The material on the Kalapooians, and particularly the Twalatine Indians, comes from Harold Mackey, PhD. (1974) and other sources, including Harvey Scott and Charles H. Carey. Data on the Clark mission with the Twalatines is enlarged as Atkinson writes in his journal of Harvey Clark's description of his early endeavors on the south and east plains, filled in by Smith's daily notes.

In this setting, the future of the Clark mission must have looked good. Clark and Littlejohn went to Vancouver, returning a week later with "4 oxen, 2 cows and 2 calves." Again, Littlejohn decided to go back East.

The temporary camp was moved November 1st to the spot where they would build near the Twalatine Indian camp. Five days later, Smith raised his log house and hired "some boys to work for us a month for 18 dolls [sic] cash price beginning next Monday." Finally, a beginning had been made.

Clark and Smith went to the Falls, and Alvin Smith saw to "buying 93 bushels of wheat & having it ground." Harvey Clark did not return with him. Instead, he began to move around and get acquainted with the country and the people. He soon became a familiar figure in his frock coat as he traveled on horseback, with a red blanket across his saddle that he might roll up in with some comfort wherever he might be as night fell.

From November 13 to December 25, Alvin Smith worked on the property. Littlejohn returned from the Whitman mission (not having gone further east) on the 25th, bringing letters from Clark. At least Harvey Clark was keeping Smith informed as to his whereabouts.

The new year was to be decisive and filled with events. It began with the positive note by Alvin Smith that he hauled lumber to the log house he was building so he could begin laying floors and put in door and window frames. An Indian brought some letters from Clark in mid-January.

In the meantime, Harvey Clark was building friendships and thinking about his education project. He had met Rev. Jason Lee, and found that they shared many of the same ideas, such as educating the Indians and bringing religion to those moving into the country.

One historian relates that Clark taught temporarily in the Methodist Indian school begun by Lee at French Prairie. The "Chronicles of Willamette" verifies this fact.

On January 17, 1842, Harvey Clark attended a meeting at the home of Jason Lee, at which plans were made to organize a school for settlers' children. Clark was the only non-Methodist member of the committee when the Salem site of the school was chosen. This became the Oregon Institute, which grew to become Willamette University.

While there had been many new experiences in Clark's travels, he was actually away from his new home for less than five months, from November 9, 1841, to March 19, 1842. The day Clark appeared, Smith reported "the wind onroofed [sic] my house." The next day being Sunday, Clark preached. The Littlejohns, Smiths and Emeline Clark were his congregation. There is no record as to whether or not Indians also attended.

On Monday morning, Alvin Smith expressed his unhappiness at the beginning of this mission. Apparently, as he worked alone he had been considering the many things that were not taking place. He wrote, "conversed with Br C & L whether to break up or not."

Two days later, Alvin Smith reopened the matter, by conversing with Mr. Clark and Mr. Littlejohn. "And," he wrote, "I concluded as Br C & Br L were so faithless about accomplishing anything for the Indians & as they were so unstable about pushing the object ahead that it is best to break up & we agreed to do so."

Smith had vented his irritation in his suggestion to close the enterprise, and there the matter rested. Clark continued to preach on the Sabbath, and Smith was in his congregation. He also made two trips to Vancouver, probably for supplies, which only Dr. John McLoughlin would have.

On July 1st, Smith "halled logs for Br Clark's house," and this continued for six days. Then came the placing of roof joists and, on October 3, they "raised the Clark house." On October 17, Smith could say, "finished the house." While Smith's diary is the only source for this journal of daily activity, it is fair to think that Clark and Littlejohn shared in the labor of construction.

During this time, the Indians in the area were becoming concerned. The Twalatines were not a large band, and they sensed that the tide of newcomers was making their life uncertain. There were not as many fish available because the settlers encroached on the supply in the streams; vegetation, like the camas, which grew wild and was basic to their diet, was disappearing; the deer were not as plentiful as they had been. Often, they were hungry.

Smith's diary chronicles some incidents involving the band, perhaps as a result of these changes:

Oct 31 hunted Indians that had stolen wheat & found 2 & brought them home, but they got away at night.

Nov 1 tended to the affairs of the Indians.

There was also the incident of the old ox which belonged to a settler. It had been killed and eaten by Indians. Of course, the owner of the old ox was irate and reported it to the Indian Sub-Agent, Dr. Elijah White.

On November 11, Dr. White came and checked into the Indian difficulties. He held a counsel with members of the band, who confessed that they had killed and eaten the animal because they were so hungry.

All these things did not make the idea of a mission at this spot feasible.

The raising of Clark's house made it necessary for him to work hard to make the interior comfortable. He stayed home, worked on the place and preached every Sunday. At stated times, Clark went to Wallamut Falls to preach to the five Protestants who needed him.

As the year drew to its end, Alvin Smith "tended a meeting of the Tualatin plains to take into consideration the making of a road to the Wallamette River." No longer were the settlers content with trails.

On December 26, problems concerning the mission rapidly came to a head. Perhaps they had been postponed until the Clark house was finished; perhaps Clark had hoped problems would disappear of their own accord. But now two groups of Kalapooian Indians were arguing about which group would control the area, and it became clear that there would not be a satisfactory Indian mission.

Griffin had earlier taken upon himself the responsibility of recording deaths and births in the area. Since there was no government, he had also taken on the power of a jurist whenever counseling was needed. Accordingly, Smith wrote:

1842 Dec 26 Br. Griffin came according to Mr. Clark's & my agreement to leave out and settle our differences & to value our improvements on this place which we agree to submit to him & we spent the remainder of the day in conversation respecting it.

Dec 27 spent today upon the same subject but did not come to a conclusion of the whole matter

Dec 29 Br Griffin came over & we attended to Br Clark's and my affairs but did not finish

Dec 30 attended to the same business & settled in part so far as the improvements are concerned I take the improvements & pay Mr. Clark 170 dollars the first payment one year from date. 36.55 dollars. the 2nd ditto two years from date 66.66 dollars. the third ditto three years from date 55.66 dollars....

I take the white cow & her calf that we had from the fort & the spotted cows last spring calf & pay him 19 dollars. I take the pair of bulls that we bought of Mr. Raymond & pay Mr. Clark 4 dollars for 1/2 the growth of them. I take the colt that we bought of Mr. Littlejohn & pay Mr. Clark 12.50 dollars. the wheat, potatoes & peas we divide, the two hogs also.

Dec 31 attended to the same & finished settling our concerns mostly & so it appears as the year closes we close up our mission concerns break up and separate so closes up this year of Our Lord 1842.

As the distribution was concluded, Griffin meticulously and most legally made his detailed report, beginning with the time the party left Quincy, Illinois, when Clark thought their property was to be one in stock and interest, and Smith thought he would control his own assets in the mission. It is an interesting document, both for its historical value and for the insights it lends to this melancholy conclusion to the year 1842.

Chapter 5
North Tualatin Plain: 1843-1844

With the mission to the Indians on the East Plain dissolved and the property in Smith's hands, it was necessary for Harvey Clark to find a new location. He chose the North Tualatin Plain, a distance above Griffin's location, on Dairy Creek. Here, some of the earlier traders from Fort Vancouver had retired, and they welcomed the Clarks.

One of the trails from the plains to Fort Vancouver led to the Wallamut Falls (now Oregon City) and north to the fort. The second trail led more directly north of the Griffin home, through a pass later called the Cornelius Pass, across the Tualatin Plain and over to Fort Vancouver.

By January 10, 1843, Smith noted that they had "settled most our concerns I hope." And, on January 12th, Smith "went and helped Br. Clark with my team to get his goods across dairy creek."

Smith and Clark had made the division of all wheat and potatoes by mid-April 1843. Alvin Smith remained on East Plain with the two cabins. Clark either built a cabin or found one in which to live and hold school classes.

The members of the Clark church were white, with Scotch background, and of mixed parentage, through Indian and white intermarriage. It had become apparent to Clark that it was nearly impossible to have a purely Indian school. However, the Clarks did attract some Indian children as well as those of mixed parentage. There was no tuition for their education, and it bears the distinction of being the first free school on the Tualatin Plain. Both Mr. and Mrs. Clark taught, and Dr. Elijah White, sub-Indian agent, reported to Washington, D.C., on April 1, 1843: "There is a small school established at Tualatin Plain by Rev. Harvey Clark and lady."[1]

William Gray reported to the American Board in Boston:

On the 16th of April last Rev. Harvey Clark organized a Presbyterian Church with 8 male & 6 female members. There is also a small church of the Congregational order in the colony. Rev. Mr. Griffin is its pastor.[2]

Clark continued occasional preaching in a settler's cabin at Wallamut Falls, although there were only three regular attendants. He was also made administrator of the Cornelius Rogers property, "descharging [sic] that duty faithfully and I think without compensation."[3]

The ministry of Clark and his fellow ministers went beyond Sabbath preaching. It carried over into legal advice, administration of property and handling other unexpected questions in the absence of government. The accidental drowning of Cornelius Rogers and his bride was a shock to their friends. Rogers had come west with the missionaries in 1838 and was popular at the Falls.

As the Rogers were about to bring their boat ashore one day, it capsized and she and her husband were pulled over the Falls. Both died in the accident.

Clark and Griffin clashed soon after the Clarks moved to the North Plain. Griffin refused to welcome those families of mixed marriage—or no marriage at all—in his church. Yet, many of the early settlers were married to, or living with, Indian wives according to the custom of the frontier.

Clark felt the families of mixed marriage should be recognized and accepted. They lived upright and faithful lives and cared for their children, and he welcomed them into his church. By the end of the year, Clark's church had more than doubled to thirty members.

As settlers moved into the valley in increasing numbers, one of the chief concerns was the need for a government. Neither Great Britain nor the United States, however, was ready to create a crisis as to ownership of this new land. Better to wait, they felt, until the time was ripe for a decision. The settlers did not agree and regularly renewed their pressure on Washing-

---

1 White, Elijah. White as sub-Indian agent in the Oregon Territory was responsible for reporting to Washington.
2 Gray, William H., vol. 248, Oregon Historical Society.
3 Cornelius Rogers had come west in 1838 with the second group of missionaries. He ran the press sent to the mission group from Hawaii, setting down the Indian dialect phonetically at the Whitman mission. He had come to the Falls to live before his sudden drowning and that of his bride.

ton. Clark and Smith knew about past requests for a government, and debate kept the matter active. In fact, Clark was soon to become an active participant in civic life of the Oregon country as he entered that growing debate.

In 1839, a petition had been sent to Washington, asking for government under United States law. There was no response. In 1840, a second petition, signed by seventy Willamette Valley residents, was sent, again asking for government. It too was ignored.

On February 7, 1841, a meeting had been held at Champoeg to consider adopting a code of laws. Nothing was concluded at the meeting, but Rev. Jason Lee preached. One of the men attending that meeting was Ewing Young, the young man who had come up from California with Hall Kelley in 1834 and settled on land along the Willamette River in the Champoeg area.

A week later, on February 15, 1841, Young died, leaving quite a bit of property. No one knew whether there was an heir, but an administrator to the estate was needed and there was no government. Jason Lee presided at a meeting following Young's funeral, and a committee of seven was selected to draft a constitution.

Allowing for no further delays, a meeting was held the next day at the Methodist mission. A committee on organization was chosen, with Father Blanchet of the Catholic mission serving as chairman. Dr. Ira Babcock of the Methodist missionary group was chosen a supreme judge with probate powers. The Laws of New York would be the basis of government.

On April 15, 1841, Dr. Babcock appointed Rev. David Leslie of the Methodist mission to administer the Young property. It looked at that time as if a government would at last become a reality when the committee on organization met June 1, 1841.

The meeting was called near the Catholic church, now St. Paul's, near Jason Lee's mission. But, surprisingly, Father Blanchet reported he had never called his committee together; he said he was not in favor of an organization. Later, he said he had not opposed organization, but that the time was inopportune. The committee was asked to confer with Dr. McLoughlin and Commodore Charles Wilkes, an explorer with the United States Army who had charted and mapped many areas and who could be helpful. The committee was scheduled to make a report in October.

At the October meeting, the report was that both Wilkes and McLoughlin advised against any further plans for organization. Why? Most of the settler population, they said, was Catholic, and they could take care of their own problems. Also, scant population meant there was no law needed for the officers to enforce. They had lived this long without law and got along well. The U.S. would eventually come along and take care of them.

It is true that the population of settlers in the Willamette Valley in 1841 was about 137 people, including 34 women and children. Here the matter rested; there would have to be a need for common ground before a government could be formed.

This was the impasse that the Clarks, Griffins and Smiths found when they moved into the valley. In Wallamut Falls, the circulating library and debating society became very active around this subject of government in 1842 and 1843. Many were the discussions, some for an independent state, some for no government at all until the United States furnished it.

Unexpected "common ground" soon surfaced on which all could agree. Wolves, lynx, bears and panthers began to encroach on the farms, especially the Ewing Young property where the livestock was now unattended. A committee canvassed the thinly populated neighborhoods and called a meeting in February 1843 to discuss the danger and find a solution. The American population now numbered almost 250, but was still widely scattered. A second meeting was held at the Gervais home. They were called the wolf meetings, and it was the first positive step in organizing a government born of necessity.

James O'Neal presided. He had been a member of Wyeth's expedition of 1832 and had brought west some law books and a copy of the statutes of Iowa. Since both Clark and Smith were very concerned and active in the government process, we can be sure they attended the wolf meetings.

Under O'Neal's leadership, the settlers got down to business by setting a price for killing the marauding animals. A bounty of 50 cents was to be paid for a small wolf, $3.00 for a large wolf, $1.50 for a lynx and $5.00 for a panther. If Indians were to kill the animals, they would receive half of what the white man would get. And, to defray these costs, each settler would be assessed $5.00.

A resolution was then made "to appoint a committee of 12" to consider measures for "civil and military protection of this colony." One of the committee of twelve was Etienne Lucier, a retired Hudson's Bay man. The committee met at Wallamut Falls and called a meeting to be held at Champoeg on May 2, 1843.

It was natural to choose Champoeg for these meetings because it was "the center or seat of the principal settlement." The settlers in the Tualatin Plains were eager to see action. Before the meeting took place, Griffin and other leaders had gone about the communities in their area, explaining what the meeting was about and urging all to come and take part, regardless of whether or not they were American settlers or the French-Canadian retirees of the Hudson's Bay Company.

Then, as now, Champoeg was a beautiful open area, shaded by heavy trees on the bank of the Willamette River. It is easy to imagine these settlers following trails to Champoeg, a few at a time, some on horseback from across the river, others from the north or south, gathering for the most important organizational meeting concerning their new lives.

Dr. Babcock was chairman of the meeting and saw that the committee report was read. Many felt that since the committee had been well-chosen—representing American and British (that is French-Canadian) subjects, Catholic and Protestant interests—the matter should be resolved easily.

The political organization was offered to them as one which would continue until such time as the United States would establish a territorial government. But this suggested to some of the British subjects that they must renounce their allegiance to Great Britain and acknowledge this as United States territory. In voting on the motion to adopt this report, a division was created that seemed to follow nationalistic lines. Dr. Babcock could not be sure which group held the majority.

Seeing the hesitation taking place, Joseph Meek, mountain man and trapper, jumped forward and took over the situation. As reported by Harvey Scott, Meek said, "Who's for a divide? All for the report of the committee and an organization, follow me."[4] The men stepped forward on either side of an area and were counted. Fifty-two voted for the provisional government; fifty against.

There is another story, not verified historically but interesting, concerning the closeness of this vote. Before this meeting in May, Etienne Lucier had told a friend he was afraid of an American government because he had heard that the U.S. had a large tax on glass for windows. His friend assured Lucier that this was not true. As a result, Lucier was one of the French-Canadians whose vote went for the provisional government.

Among those voting for the government were Harvey Clark, Alvin Smith and John Griffin who had so recently made their way to the Willamette Valley. Also voting for the government were William H. Gray of

---

4   Scott, Harvey W. Some said dramatically that Meek drew a heavy line in the dirt to designate the two sides for voting. Among the Griffin papers I found in the Oberlin Alumni file was a letter in which Griffin said he made a speech that influenced the vote about to be taken. It is probable that many voices were heard on that momentous occasion.

Whitman's party arriving in 1836, Robert Moore, who came west in 1840; David Hill, for whom Hillsboro is named; and others who in later years would become more involved with Harvey Clark.[5]

It had been decided wisely that clergymen should not hold positions in the formation of the new government, but their advice was sought. Rev. Harvey Clark's name, along with that of Rev. Jason Lee, appear as consultants:

> Resolved, that the president of the convention assisted by the Rev. Messrs. Lee, Clark and Leslie, be a committee to draft and administer an oath of office to the civil officers elected on the 2nd of May 1843....[6]

On July 5, 1843, again meeting at Champoeg, the officers elected on May 2 were sworn into office. The territory was divided into four districts: Twality District; Yamhill District; the Champooick [sic] District; and the Clackamas District, which would take in all country not in the other districts.

Other matters were also settled at this important meeting which followed the Iowa legal statutes as the start of the new provisional government. Among the matters, Alvin Smith was named magistrate for the Twality District. At the conclusion of the sessions, the settlers felt satisfied that a good beginning had been made.

Ministers still had their churchly duties and on July 12, 1843, "the Methodist camp meeting in Oregon was at or near Hillsboro. The Rev. Jason Lee conducted services. Other ministers present were Gustavus Hines, H.K.W. Perkins, David Leslie and Harvey Clark."[7] Dr. Marcus Whitman was impressed by the report on Lee's meetings, and passed on the news in a letter to the American Board in Boston, also including Clark's progress on Tualatin Plain:

> Mr. Jason Lee was in a most interesting state of mind. He had just come in from a series of religious meetings among the settlers of the Willamette. I think great good is doing by them [the missionaries] among the Settlers. Mr. Clark also has a prosperous Church but Mr. Griffin seems to be doing little

---

5   Dobbs, Carolyn, *Men of Champoeg.*

6   The Oregon Archives, July 5, 1843.

7   Whitman, Marcus, writing to the American Board on a camp meeting he attended under Jason Lee's leadership.

or no good.

An early provision ought to be made for schools in this country.

Marcus Whitman[8]

The group that came west in 1843 was large, and the emigrant population of the entire Oregon Country now swelled to nearly 1,200 people. The need for educational facilities was being felt more keenly. The schools were given an important place in Dr. Elijah White's report to Washington, D.C. in November of that year:

> There are now four schools kept in the colony: one at Falatine Plains, under
> the direction and auspices of the Rev. Mr. Clark, a self-supporting
> missionary; a second (French and English) school is a successful operation
> by Mr. Blanchet, Roman Catholic missionary to this colony; a third is
> well-sustained by the citizens and kept at the falls of the Willamet; a
> fourth...by the Methodists for the benefit of the Indian youth.[9]

In closing his report for 1843, Dr. White gave recommendations for future emigrant travelers, and closed with these words:

> Have no apprehension of want; it is a land of plenty.... At our Oregon
> Lyceum it was unanimously voted that the colony of Willamette held out the
> most flattering encouragement to immigrants of any colony on the globe.[10]

With the beginning of the new year, 1844, the Clarks were busy, teaching and preaching on the North Plain. The Smiths had moved to the West Plain, six miles away, south of the present site of Forest Grove. (The Smiths' home was about where the Carnation Mill now stands.) Mr. and Mrs. Littlejohn had gone back to Lapwai with the Spaldings. Of the six who had come west in 1840, only the Clarks were still pursuing the mission-school project he had preached about so earnestly in 1839 and 1840.

---

8   *Ibid.*
9   White, Elijah. He refers to "Falatine Plain." Later, Carey calls it Tualatin
     Plain.
10   *Ibid.*

At the Falls, where Clark ministered as he could find time, three men talked about starting a church. On May 24, 1844, the church was organized by Rev. Clark, with Peter Hatch, a Congregationalist from Massachusetts; Robert Moore, a Presbyterian who had come west in 1840 with the Clark group; and Osborne Russell, a Baptist from Maine and a long-time trapper. When it came to naming the church, Robert Moore wanted them to be Presbyterian, and since he was the oldest man, "venerable and of strong convictions," it became The Presbyterian Church of Wallamut Falls.[11] Mr. Clark continued as minister, coming at stated Sundays for the next four years, in addition to his work on the North Plain.

Clark began a series of temperance meetings, feeling that they were needed because of the growing population. Smith attended the "Temperance meetings," but on Sundays "Br Griffin preached" at the Smith home.

When Clark had preached in the North Plain for a year and a half, there was trouble in the church. It was only much later that Clark wrote in a report to the Congregational Home Mission Society the details of the problem he faced at the time. A part of his report follows, explaining his dejection:

> After a year and a half of prosperity the church in Tualatin Plains at a wedding after the Scotch custom, had a dance which almost broke it up. At this time the church numbered 25 members mostly half bloods. I felt most sensibly the need of aid and counsel. It seemed that if God in his providence did not send help from some quarter I myself must soon leave the field. It is true a number of ministers came of other denominations but not to do all that was necessary and urgently demanded.

The specifics of this problem are not known. Probably it was a case of dancing, which was frowned upon, and drinking and hilarity. This might have been handled by Clark, but Griffin was a very critical man and too expressive in his opinions, which created added tension.

Disheartened as Clark was, he could get no help or comfort from Griffin, who felt Clark's church was too near his own and who did not believe in ministering to those of mixed marriage as Clark did. Clark's letter continues:

> After a few months labor in doing all I could to reclaim those who had strayed I concluded to return to the states thinking it was not my duty to bear

---

11   Centennial History of the Congregational Church, Oregon City.

such responsibilities alone and with so little hope of ultimate success. This the providence of God did not permit.[12]

While Harvey Clark was healing the members of his church, Alvin Smith on the West Plain faced his own problems. Those had to do with possession. Smith had not set stakes showing his land-claim boundaries. The new territorial law just voted emphasized that either blazes on trees or stakes at corners must be used to show lines of possession.

On October 9, 1844, Smith noted that a man named Reeves was ignoring Smith's land claim, and Smith "forbade his trespassing any more on my claim." Reeves ignored the warning. Belatedly, on October 29, Smith set the corner stakes on his claim. The next day, Smith asked three men to come over from the East Plain "to settle a question about my claim between me and Reeves." (We might note the extent of his pique, in that Smith did not refer to Reeves as "Mr." or "Br.," the usual titles in that more formal time.) The men he called were David Hill, Williams and Wilkins. All agreed with Smith. On November 2, Smith's diary stated, "I gave him [Reeves] notice to leave within ten days or suffer the consequences." At this point, Reeves moved off the Smith claim. Incidents like this showed how much people in such situations needed a law for protection.

Village centers were taking root. David Hill, a member of the group at Champoeg in 1843, had settled on the East Plain, naming the place Columbus. Here he built a general store. As time passed, in spite of Hill's choice of place name, people insisted on going to "Hill's borough" to shop or pick up their mail. Finally, it became Hillsboro.

The year 1844 also saw a marked change in tension with the Indians. Where earlier the settlers had enjoyed a sense of security, the increasing number of arrivals caused the Indians to become increasingly concerned. They attacked Wallamut Falls, they appeared to threaten Chemetka and they threatened the Oregon Institute.

The people on the Tualatin Plains waited for the Indians to threaten them, yet no threat appeared. It may have been because there were fewer Twalatine Indians as well as fewer residents. The Indians wandered around, often hungry because there was less camas and other vegetable foods, the streams did not provide as many fish, and others were getting the deer.

The impact on Indians' food sources was seen in incidents like the one Emeline Clark faced one morning. Mrs. Clark was outside her cabin, hav-

12   Hammond Library.

ing just put her small baby in a basket by the door. Looking up, she saw an Indian coming into the clearing from the woods. He asked for food. She answered that she had nothing. He said, "Then I kill baby," and he stepped toward the sleeping child, her first-born. Emeline moved quickly. She got a broom from just inside the door and brandished it in the air, shouting as she came toward him. He turned and ran into the woods with her following him to the edge of the clearing.[13] It was one of the many unsettling experiences they learned to live with at that time.

Other local concerns on the West Plain attracted Alvin Smith. He helped build a bridge to make travel easier. And, he helped a neighbor north of him, Orus Brown, "run out his claim." (Orus Brown had come west in 1833, found the West Plain good, and settled, planning to return east later to get his family.)

In November 1844, Dr. Elijah White again reported to the United States on the state of the Oregon Country, including the schools:

> The schools at the falls of the Willamette and Falatine plains are all
> small...numbering from fifteen to thirty [students] only, but are well kept and
> doing good.[14]

---

13 Platt, Miss Helen, great-granddaughter of Emeline Clark, in an interview with the author.

14 White, Elijah.

Chapter 6
Tualatin Plains: 1845-1847

Alvin Smith liked his new home on the West Plain. He had good neighbors, and he felt it would be a good year. He helped Orus Brown, his neighbor to the north, raise his house. He also helped a neighbor to the west, Thomas Naylor, put up his house and worked on Naylor's bridge.

But he did have problems with the Indians. On February 8, Smith noted that he "went to the other plain to hunt for my horse the Indians drove away." Not until February 11th did he get back his stolen horse.

In spite of the physical labor at hand, Alvin Smith's mind was also at work on some new ideas. There were enough people on the West Plain to make Smith believe it was time to plan for a church. On March 17th, he mounted his horse and rode to the East Plain to talk to John Griffin, who had been preaching at the Smith cabin for a year. He wrote:

> Went over to Br Griffin and held a consultation about inviting Br Clark to
> come to this plain to settle and preach for us half of the time.

Harvey Clark expressed interest in the suggestion when he was approached by Smith. The only drawback was that it meant moving to the West Plain and he did not see how he could raise the money for housing.

A solution came quickly. Orus Brown was about to leave for the States to get his family and agreed to sell Clark his land claim and log house for 500 bushels of wheat, payable after the harvest when he returned from the East.[1] The land was good and productive, and the venture would be a safe

---

1   Lewis, Mrs. H.A., Portland, in a letter to the author in 1948.

one. Harvey Clark accepted the offer and prepared to leave the church on the North Plain.

In April, Smith "helpt Mr. Brown about getting ready for the states," but it was not until June 21 that the Orus Brown party left for the East. At that same time, those on the West Plain held a meeting to dismiss Griffin, their pastor. On June 22, Clark preached his first sermon at the Geiger school. This is the only mention of Geiger's school and it must have been for private pupils since Dr. Elijah White's reports do not mention it.

Again, government affairs intruded into the pastor's daily life, for at the Provisional legislative committee meeting in Oregon City, William Gray made a motion: "Resolved that the morning session of this House be commenced with prayer."[2] This was on June 24. The legislative committee accepted the resolution and balloted for a person to officiate as chaplain. Rev. H. Clark was their choice, and the next day he opened the session with prayer.[3]

On June 31, 1845, the church called Harvey Clark to be the pastor on the West Tualatin Plain, believing that before too long a building would be necessary for services. By 1845 the population had doubled; 3,000 new settlers were reported, arriving late in the season and in most cases with little money. As a result, barter became the medium of exchange. But with this influx of settlers, it was certain a cabin would not be big enough to hold worship services.

With the growing population on the West Plain, a community began to take shape and links with other communities were strengthened. In 1846, Stephen Meek ran an ad in the *Oregon Spectator*: "Telegraph Line with Eight Ox Power. Semi-weekly service between Oregon City and Tualatin Plain settlements. Rain or no rain, mud or no mud, load or no load, but not without pay."

The legislative committee, from now on called the House, struggled with the requests for roads between settlements. Each of the four districts wanted roads, and ferries and bridges across rivers. One request from Twality was for a county seat. The House let the Twality District vote for it, and the decision was in favor of Columbus, the town founded by David Hill. This meant the lawyers in Portland had to come to Columbus (later to be named Hillsboro) to try their cases after the August 5th vote.

---

2   The Oregon Archives.

3   *Ibid.*

As an aside, it is interesting to note the expanse of the Twality District, or county, included "all land south of the northern boundary line of the United States, west of the Willamette, or Multnomah River north of the Yamhill River, and east of the Pacific Ocean."[4] This had been approved by the people on July 5, 1843.

With the departure of Orus Brown, the Clarks settled themselves in their new home just north of the Smiths. There, Clark set about raising crops, as Smith and virtually every settler did since growing one's own food was a prime necessity. But, not far from his mind was a church building to house his flock. As Clark reported to the American Missionary Society in the East:

> I with a few brethren (white) in another part of Tualatin began again; and most of the half-blood church (from the North Plain) united with us. We increased to some 30 (members) and a large and prosperous Sabbath School.[5]

The Littlejohns had returned to West Tualatin in the fall and Smith helped haul logs for the construction of the Littlejohn house. He also worked "on the bridge at David Hill's" that fall. In mid-October, Smith helped "Mr. Clark on his house", and on November 27 "helpt Br Clark raise his house."

Church services continued at the Clark cabin, with him preaching and Alvin Smith a regular attendant. Harvey Clark shared his ideas about a church with Smith, Geiger and Naylor. It was decided to put a building in the northern part of the Clark land claim. The ground was high and level and there was a good setting of oak trees. Between the upper and lower sections of the Clark claim ran a "slough," low land that was wet and boggy, which necessitated a foot bridge for crossing.

On May 30, 1846, they raised the meeting house. It must have caused a great deal of excitement and satisfaction, for it was the first church building in the Oregon Country. The building measured 25 feet by 40 feet, and was built of logs plastered with mud. At one end was a fireplace for warmth, and at the other end a door. A window was centered on each side to give light. The seats were made of puncheons, or half logs. Since Clark wanted a school as well as a church, they put half logs on the side walls for the older

---

4   *Ibid.*
5   Hammond Library.

students to use as desks and benches on school days. The floor, too, was of half logs. The total cost was $30.00 for the meeting house, thanks to the volunteer help that did the actual construction.[6]

With the meeting house raised and the weather clear, Clark and Smith immediately planned for their first camp meeting. The ground had to be selected, with an area open enough to accommodate wagons and sleeping arrangements because those who came from a distance would make camp. Also, a cooking area had to be set up, along with a worship center for preaching. On June 2, they chose a section of Naylor's woods, west of the Smith claim. On June 8 and 9, they worked on the camp ground, on the 10th "killed a Beef for camp meeting." They were ready when the meeting opened to run from June 11 through the 22nd.

The meeting must have been successful, for while there were no figures showing attendance or souls saved, Smith reported on the camp meeting:

June 11-22 Had a good meeting & felt the power of God as I never felt it before.

On September 22, Smith went to Vancouver and settled all with the Hudson's Bay Company & paid them for the Rev Harvey Clark thirty one dollars and forty three cents which is all the demand the said Clark has against me by note.

This represented the final payment due on the Mission project in the South Plain. Smith's payments had been regularly paid when due, as he mentioned in his diary. It was probably a real joy to be able to say "finished" to the payments.

In the fall, the Smith diary reports he attended church services "at Br Littlejohns," which might make one wonder if again Smith was disapproving of Clark. That was not the case. Clark was ill. Hearing of the illness, Dr. Whitman had invited the Clarks to winter with them at Waiilatpu and expected them to accept the invitation. Harvey Clark improved, however, and did not make the visit to his friend.

November and December 1846 found Smith continuing to work on the meeting house. Orus Brown returned in September with a horrifying tale of being attacked and robbed by a group of Pawnee Indians 400 miles from the

---

6   Walker and Eells, students writing later of their experiences.

United States frontier. He and three other men with him had lived on berries and rosebuds until they were able to reach the frontier settlement.

Brown had met his family, then been appointed as a wagon train pilot, so he was separated from his relatives on the trip west. But he said he was not worried about his family, who were traveling six days behind his group. The party consisted of his brother-in-law, Virgil Pringle, his five children, and his wife and mother. When word finally came that a party had attempted the cutoff, or shortcut, across the mountains, Orus Brown became frantic. He knew the cutoff was dangerous and was never recommended, and he was fearful that his family was in danger. On November 22, Brown left his friends on the West Plain to try to contact his family.

Only later did the Clarks and Smiths learn the details of Brown's search. Orus Brown started toward the cutoff and met his brother-in-law, Pringle, who was coming for help. Together they retraced Pringle's trail to the lost immigrants. On Christmas Day, 1846, the weary party finally entered Salem, after nine months of grueling travel, hunger and distress.[7]

With the beginning of the new year, 1847, Harvey Clark's health improved and he held regular church services in his home until the new meeting house would be finished. Clark was eagerly waiting for the printed material promised through Dr. Whitman for the Clark project. One of the weaknesses in the new West was the dearth of reading materials, and the Bible and Tract Society in Boston was sending $100 worth to be sold or distributed to parishioners and neighbors. In addition, the Massachusetts Sabbath School Society promised a grant for Clark's Sunday School program. Since all these materials had to come around the continent and through Honolulu, no one knew when they might arrive.

On April 8, Alvin Smith and Harvey Clark went to the new town of Portland on a direct road, which had finally been constructed from the West Plain. At last the communities seemed to be coming closer to each other. The next day, the books arrived from Honolulu and Smith "assisted Br Clark to see to his books." Clark was overjoyed at the gift from Massachusetts.

The P.B. Littlejohns had talked longingly of returning to their home in the East almost from the time of their arrival at the Whitmans' in 1840. At last it became possible, and on April 29, Alvin Smith "helpt Br and Sister Littlejohn to start for the states." The Littlejohns were among the few who

---

7   Brown, Tabitha: Letter detailing the hazards she and an elderly uncle, John, faced on the cut-off from the trail. Pacific University Library.

could not take the rigors of the untamed West, nor could they find a niche in which to fit in the new communities that were being born.

Clark missed his friend, for Littlejohn had been helpful in preaching when Clark was sick. Clark continued his full schedule of preaching, teaching at his school with his wife, when she had time, and farming for a livelihood. The Clarks had been blessed with a child in 1844, while living on the North Plain. She was a girl whom they named Satira Emeline, and this easily explains why the teaching fell more heavily on Harvey's shoulders at times.

Earlier, for short periods of time, Smith had kept one or two children as boarders in his home so they could attend the Clark school. On May 21, Smith opened his home again, noting:

> Mr. Owens brought his nieces here to stay until they are each of them 18 years of age to be kept and managed as our own children.

On July 30, help arrived from an unexpected source in the form of Rev. Cornwall. The family had come west in the 1846 migration, hoping to file a claim in Chehalem Valley. The land was all taken up, and having heard of the West Tualatin Plain, he came to see if there might be a place for him. Alvin Smith brought Cornwall to see Harvey Clark, and together the men encouraged Cornwall to move to the Plain. Smith went to help move the Cornwalls, and Clark furnished a cabin for a temporary home.

The Cornwall cabin was probably the new one Smith was helping Clark build, because his daughter Narcissa Cornwall described it as "unfinished, with no fireplace or cookstove." Because of this, they cooked their meals outside as they had done coming west. Narcissa explained how well her father adapted to the situation:

> Father soon began teaching. I don't think he ever received a dollar in money but we were supplied with vegetables, meat and flour. Either father or Dr. Clark preached every Sunday and they kept a Sabbath school, Dr. Geiger being superintendant.[8]

Cornwall fitted easily into the environment, and furnished relief to the overworked Br. Clark. The church membership began to grow, with the addition of "12 new members, 2 by profession," according to the Smith diary.

---

8   Lockley, Fred.

When Dr. Marcus Whitman and his nephew, Perrin, came to the Clarks' for a short visit, he was glad to meet the Cornwalls, for they represented the needed leadership in both church and education in the growing communities.

In the conversation, Mrs. Cornwall asked Dr. Whitman if his wife was not afraid to live among the Indians. He said that Mrs. Whitman's answer was always the same, "The Indians never killed women."[9] However, he admitted that they did have some uneasiness in Waiilatpu. McLoughlin had been warning the Whitmans since 1843 that he did not think they should trust the Cayuse Indians and would do well to move to the Willamette Valley.

Dr. Whitman had even talked to Clark about coming south eventually and working with him in some capacity; and only that spring, Mrs. Whitman had written to Mrs. Smith that if the Indians did not want them there any longer, she and her husband looked forward to coming to West Tualatin.

Upon returning to Waiilatpu, Dr. Whitman wrote an exciting letter to the Mission House in Boston, asking for more workers in the new communities in the Willamette area—mechanics and manufacturers were now needed, as well as ministers and educators.

The reply, written October 21, 1847, probably never reached Dr. Whitman before tragedy struck those at the Mission. If it did, he had no time to relay the good news to his friend, Harvey Clark. Mr. Greene of the Mission House said a man and his wife were just leaving the East on their way to the Oregon Teritory. His name was Rev. George Henry Atkinson, and he was coming by way of Honolulu, representing the Congregational Home Missionary Society. This was indeed good news.[10]

Despite increasing tensions between the missionaries and the Cayuse, the attack on the Mission was unexpected. There was no warning when Cayuse men broke into the Mission, killing the Whitmans and others. Fortunately, some of the residents made an escape, although many more were taken prisoner. A very few were away from the Mission at the time of the attack.

The tragedy cast its long shadow on the Tualatin Plain. Cornwall's daughter reported:

---

9   *Ibid.*

10   Hurlbert & Hurlbert, *Marcus Whitman, Crusader*, American Board letter, also in the Houghton Library.

The news came that Dr. and Mrs. Whitman had been murdered and a runner came to our house in the night and called Father and asked if he had a gun. He answered that he had a gun and two large pistols. He told them to keep them loaded and be prepared to protect his family, as they were expecting Indians to attack the settlers any night.[11]

While the massacre at the Whitman Mission happened on November 29 and 30, the news didn't reach the Cornwalls, Clarks and Smiths until December 9. On December 10, the Smith diary relates:

Wife was called to Mr. Cornwall's & news that Doct Whitman & wife & 10 other men at their station were murdered by the Indians.

The settlers on the Plain knew this called for action. They had no way of knowing whether they would be next. Smith wrote:

Dec 14 tended a meeting at Ebberts to take into consideration the necessity of sending men to punish the murderers of Doct Whitman & families.

Little by little, further news came to the West Plain. The other missionaries—the Spaldings, Walkers and Eells—were being evacuated from their missions for safety. They arrived at Oregon City, and the foreign mission program in the West came to an end.

The Oregon House took up the murder of the Whitmans at their meeting. After reading "a number of letters from Messrs of the forts on the Columbia, announcing the horrid murder of Dr. Whitman, family and others, accompanied by a letter from the governor, praying the immediate action of the House in the matter," the House quickly made a decision:

Resolved - That the governor [Gov. Abernethy] is hereby required to raise arms and equip a company of riflemen, not to exceed fifty men with their captain and subaltern officers, and dispatch them forthwith to occupy the mission station at the Dalles, on the Columbia River, and hold possession until reinforcements arrive.[12]

---

11 Lockley, Fred.
12 The Oregon Archives, 1843-1849.

The station at The Dalles was the Methodist mission begun by Jason Lee. It was a regular stop for travelers after leaving Fort Hall or the Whitman Mission and was a strategically important station to protect.

Events in the Willamette Valley moved ahead, in spite of the shock of the Whitman massacre and demands for a militia.

In Salem, Tabitha Brown and Capt. John, her uncle-in-law, had arrived on Christmas Day, 1846. They were resting following their rescue on the trail cutoff by Orus Brown and Virgil Pringle, Tabitha's son and son-in-law, respectively. After all, Tabitha Brown was 65 years old, and Capt. John was much older and frail.

During the spring of 1847, Tabitha, rested after her ordeal, served a family as their temporary housekeeper. Feeling fully recovered and with a curiosity about this new land she had adopted, she decided to see the country. She went by boat from Salem to Oregon City, and then down the Columbia to the Pacific. Here, she spent the summer at Clatsop Plains, a new settlement boasting just ten families. In October, on her way back to Salem, Mrs. Brown decided it would be an opportune time to pay a visit to her son, Orus, at the West Tualatin Plain.

Upon arriving at Oregon City, she hired a man with an empty wagon, who also happened to be a neighbor of Orus. He drove her to her son's home for what she anticipated would be a two-week visit.

On her first Sunday there, Orus took his mother to church where she met the minister, Harvey Clark, and his wife Emeline. It was a happy meeting, and an instant warmth developed between the Clarks and Mrs. Brown. Mrs. Brown reported on the growing friendship:

> They [the Clarks] invited me home with them to spend a few days. Winter set in; they pressed me hard to spend the winter with them. I accepted their invitation. Our intimacy ever since has been more like mother and children than strangers. They are about the same age as my own children and look to me for advice and counsel equally as much. They even think they have the greatest claim, for they insist upon my spending the balance of my days with them.[13]

Mrs. Brown was a ready listener as Clark told of his hopes, and being a person of ideas herself, she made an excellent companion for the Clarks. In the

---

13   Brown, Tabitha.

course of their conversations, Mrs. Brown expressed a few thoughts she had been nurturing:

> I said to Mr. Clark: why has providence frowned on me and left me poor in this world? Had He blessed me with riches as He has so many others, I would know right well what I should do. "What would you do?" was the question. "I should establish myself in a comfortable house, and receive all poor children and be a mother to them."

> He fixed his keen eye upon me and asked if I was candid in what I'd said. "Yes, I am." "If so, I will try with you and see what we can do."

> Mr. Clark was to take the agency, and try to get assistance to establish a school for the first in the Plain; I should go into the log meeting house and receive all the children, rich and poor. Those whose parents were able to pay $1.00 a week, including board, tuition, washing and all. I agreed to labor one year for nothing; Mr. Clark and others agreed to assist me as far as they were able in furnishing provisions, providing there was not a sufficiency of cash coming in to sustain the poor. The time fixed was March '48.[14]

While it did not take long for Mrs. Brown to relate the embryonic dream in her journal, it is natural to believe that many evenings saw these two refining their plans for the new venture. The Clark school was already functioning under Cornwall and Clark, but this would be an additional step forward—adding a boarding house and a home for orphaned children as well as an education.

As 1847 drew to a close, Gov. Abernethy sent a message to the House:

> December 1847 ....The case of education demands your attention. School districts should be formed in the several counties, and school houses built. Teachers would be employed by the people, I have no doubt, and thus pave the way for more advanced institutions.[15]

This would be something for the House, as governing body, to take up in the new year. But the recent immigrants, now numbering between "four and

---

14   *Ibid.*
15   The Oregon Archives, reports on the meeting Dec. 8, 1847.

five thousand souls", most of whom had settled in the Willamette Valley, were really not concerned about education at this moment. There were more immediate matters concerning the settlers—the danger of an Indian uprising, which would be a surprise attack when it occurred. Even more than fear was the anger they felt for the lives of friends lost at the hands of Indians they believed they were helping, and a desire for vengeance against the murderers. Alvin Smith's diary expressed it well in January 1848:

> Jan 3 loaned a horse to William Stokes to go on an expedition against the Cayuse Indians for murdering Doct Whitman

> Jan 4 loaned Alvin Brown a rifle for the same purpose as Mr Stokes the horse

> Jan 11 went to the tualatin lodge to tell the Rowlands children as they are orphans went to Hew Banks & Naylors to see if they would take some of the children, but they did not agree.

Both the Banks and the Naylors were members of the Congregational Church, and Alvin Smith thought they might be helpful, but they were not able to assist.

Organized action began to take place, as Smith wrote:

> Jan 15 went to the east plain to tend a meeting of the citizens to organize into a military capacity for defence against the Indians in case of disturbance.

There followed a series of military meetings to prepare for catastrophe if it should come to the West Plain. The settlers grew more sure each day that they would have to protect themselves. Too, they became increasingly aware of their isolation. But the Provisional Government did act. Gov. Abernethy issued an order: the military must move against the Cayuse Indians. Probably the "military" Abernethy mentioned were the volunteers from the local communities, such as the West Plain, who had been holding their military meetings.

Again, the United States government lagged, being content with having set up the Provisional Government.

One of the children at the Whitman mission was Helen Mar Meek, whose father was Joe Meek. She had been sick and died in captivity on December 7 after the massacre, and Meek held a personal grievance. Active in the Provisional Government, he hurried across country to Washington with the news of the Whitman massacre and the Cayuse War. President Polk requested that Congress act speedily on the Oregon crisis. Meek was not only a colorful character, dressed in his western clothing, but he was also a persuasive personality to whom Congress listened.

Congress' excuse for delay had been because the Southern senators wanted to wait about further voting until they could be sure of having slavery in the Oregon Country. The Whitman outrage precipitated decision, however, and the bill presented to the Senate prohibited slavery in Oregon. It was passed, and again after a long delay, the House finally approved it.

The Oregon Territory—a "free" territory—at last became fact in 1848. Joseph Lane was to be the governor, and Joe Meek was appointed United States Marshall.

News of this decision, however, did not reach the people of the Oregon Territory until Feb. 5, 1849, since word had to come by way of the Hawaiian Islands.

Illustrations

Source: Portrait of Harvey Clark. Gelatin silver print copy of an earlier photograph. Original image circa 1855. Pacific University Archives. PUApic_008009.

Harvey Clark, Congregational minister, pioneer and educator.

Alvin T. Smith, pioneer and diarist.

Joseph Lafayette "Joe" Meek, trapper for the Rocky Mountain Fur Company, territorial federal marshal and legislator in Oregon's Provisional Government.

George Henry Atkinson, missionary and educator, who helped found Pacific University while urging the creation of a public school system in Oregon.

Source: Hyde & Peirce (engravers). "Pacific University, Forest Grove, Oregon." From: *Catalog of Pacific University and Tualatin Academy*, Forest Grove, Oregon. 1867-1868. Portland, Oregon: A. G. Walling, Book & Job Printer, 1868. Image scanned by the Pacific University Archives from the copy in the Tongue Papers.

A woodcut of Pacific's campus as it appeared in 1870. At left is the church designed by Alvin Smith and (center rear) President Marsh's home.

Source: Harvey and Emeline Clark's House. Photograph. Circa 1930s[?]. Pacific University Archives. PUApic_008690.

The Clarks' home. In her dairy, Margaret Hinman stated, "It stood on 5th Street and 5th Avenue. The bush at the corner is of old fashioned roses. A sweet briar bush which stood south of the Clark home was for many years in the parking of Mrs. Watt's house (now Alpha Zeta) just at the corner of 5th and 5th. At the time of his death, Mr. Clark was living in a house not now standing on the block west of Mrs. Seymour's, which would be on 2nd Street and 2nd Avenue. The house in which he died was built by Dr. S.H. Marsh, according to his son, Wheelock, but this (log house) is the home to which Dr. George H. Atkinson came with Deacon Peter H. Hatch, from Oregon City to consult Rev. Clark about 'establishing an institution of higher learning.' The story is Rev. Clark's small daughter met Dr. Atkinson at the door to say 'Father is conducting a camp meeting' in a grove near by 'but will be home soon' which he was—when the two men of like mind laid plans for the school which is now Pacific University."

The original log church, which doubled as a classroom, was referred to affectionately as "God's Barn."

Source: Log cabins on Alvin T. Smith's land. Silver gelatin print photograph. Circa 1900-1930. Pacific University Archives. PUApic_009198.

Alvin Smith's log home and post office. In her diary, Margaret Hinman stated, "These two log cabins were on the donation claim of Alvin T. Smith and were situated south of what is known as Carnation. One [look closely for the man seated in the doorway] was the residence. The other was the first post office of Forest Grove. Within the memory of some of us (in 1948) old timers, parts of these log cabins remained on the Smith place covered over with old time roses — calico (red with white stripes) and the sweet mission rose."

Source: Pacific University advertisement. *The Weekly Oregonian*, December 1854. Estate of Walter C. Giersbach.

The Weekly Oregonian *(Portland, O.T. [Or.]) ran a classified ad in December 1854 inviting students to apply at a tuition of $32 per year.*

Pacific University's original women's dormitory, Herrick Hall, was the only student housing on campus when it was built in 1884. The University used it in marketing to female students, who were offered suites of two rooms: "a study room and a sleeping room [...] comfortably furnished with carpet, stove, study-table, wash-stand, mirror, chairs, woven wire bed with mattress, lamp and window curtains" for $3-$4 per week. (Source: Pacific University Catalogue, 1888.) The hall burned down in 1906.

Source: The Second Herrick Hall under construction. Silver gelatin print photograph. 1907. Pacific University Archives. PUA-pic_012709.

A new Herrick Hall was constructed one year after the first one was destroyed in a fire. This photograph shows its construction out of brick. Despite the safer materials, it too succumbed to fire in 1973. After that, the building was razed and never rebuilt.

Chapter 7
The Growing Period: 1848-1850

Life in the West Tualatin Plain began to take on a more settled dimension, though the threat presented by the Whitman massacre was still on the minds of the settlers. Harvey Clark had enlisted the aid of Alvin Smith in furthering his building plans. As Smith wrote:

Jan 24 halled some wood to the school house and tended a military meeting
Jan 26 Mr. Clark commenced getting out timber
Jan 27 halled logs for the Orphan Asylum

It became clear that the first institution for orphans in the Oregon Territory was about to be born.

March 26, 1848, was a special day for rejoicing, with the completion of the church building. Alvin Smith wrote, "tended meeting at the meeting house for the first time." To be sure, Smith's diary said they raised the meeting house on May 30, 1846, and its specifications were listed. But the Sunday worship continued in Clark's home because the walls had to be chinked with mud, left to dry and refilled in spots where necessary; the fireplace had to be built, windows put in, seats and desks made for the school and the church finished. This was done by March 1848. From then on, worship was held in the church instead of a settler's cabin.

Work continued on the orphan asylum as Clark and Smith built the long log house to serve as living quarters for the orphan students. Also in March, Alvin Smith accepted another child for his home:

John Terwilliger came here to board & go to school & work for his board.
Paid Mr. Clark for the books I bought of him.

In early April, Tabitha Brown left the Clarks and went back to Salem to get her belongings. There, she found that Capt. John, who had made the trip West with her, had died. His death left Mrs. Brown free to start her new life in the West Tualatin Plain. She returned on the last Saturday night of April 1848, and reported that she found the orphan house was ready for occupancy:

> The neighbors had collected together what broken knives and forks, tin pans and dishes they could part with for the Oregon Pioneer to commence housekeeping. A well educated lady from the east, a missionary's wife was the teacher.

> I had now thirty boarders of all sexes and ages, from 4 years old to 21. I managed them, did almost all of my own work, but the washing, which was always done by the students.[1]

Tabitha Brown must be given the credit for taking responsibility for the first orphan asylum in the Oregon Territory, where needy children might be given a home and motherly care. To this home came the children orphaned on the trip from the East, as well as those whose parents were now being lured to the gold fields in California. Not only could the West Plain boast a school, but a boarding school as well.

As Harvey Clark and Alvin Smith began preparation for the annual June camp meeting, they were not aware that shortly a new chapter was about to begin, bringing yet another change to the project on which they labored.

George Henry Atkinson was on his way to the Oregon Country under the Home Missionary Society in the East. He was a graduate of Dartmouth College. In 1843, upon his graduation, he enrolled at Andover Theological Seminary, planning to prepare for missionary service in foreign fields. He expressed his feeling when writing to his cousin, Josiah Hale, in March 1846:

> I know not how I can decide to remain in my own land when viewing all these things in the light of eternity.... One thing I know, I have never had

---

1   Brown, Tabitha: Typed manuscript.

more confidence in Christ than since making the decision to go and preach the gospel to the Heathen, leaving friends and all.[2]

Graduating from the seminary in June 1846, he was married in the fall to Nancy Bates. Since a friend and fellow seminarian was also interested in foreign missions, the two young couples scheduled themselves to sail for the mission in South Africa under the American Board's sponsorship. Their ship, however, arrived ahead of schedule and, before Atkinson could be ordained (a requisite for any missionary), the ship set sail with the other couple, leaving the Atkinsons behind.

George Atkinson was faced with considering other possibilities. The most interesting appeared to be the mission field in the western territory. He discussed the opportunity with Dr. Milton Badger, secretary of the Home Missionary Society and asked to be released from his obligations to the American Board since the Oregon Territory was now under the American Home Missionary Society.

In January 1847, George Atkinson wrote to his uncle, Josiah Little:

Within a few days we have concluded to go to Oregon under the Home Missionary Society, providence permitting. It will doubtless meet the approval of friends. It has caused a painful struggle to give up the hope of doing some thing in person for the degraded African. Yet we hope to be useful in that distant and destitute portion of our own country.[3]

Atkinson visited New York in May for instructions on his future work in the West. Dr. Badger introduced him to Dr. Theron Baldwin, secretary of the American College Society. The one objective of that society was to establish a college in every new state across the breadth of the country. Dr. Baldwin liked the looks of the young man and laid a responsibility upon him, saying, "You are going to Oregon. Build an academy which shall grow into a college." This responsibility, then, was added to the one given him by the Home Missionary Society—to found Congregational Churches.

Unlike previous travelers, who had dangerous, fatiguing months on the trail west, the Atkinsons had a relatively pleasant trip, sailing on the *Samoset* on October 23, 1847. The sea voyage allowed time for relaxation

---

2   Atkinson, George H.: Letters, Huntington Library.
3   *Ibid.*

and reading. It also permitted them to bring a greater amount of baggage and books than could have been carried over the land route.

The trip was not totally comfortable in some respects. When the weather was cold, the cabin was heated by a brazier or heated cannon ball "suspendent from the ceiling in a strong wire basket." One of the greatest discomforts was the lack of water. "Part of the time they were allowed only a pint a day for washing and shaving."[4]

After 125 days at sea, the Atkinsons' ship arrived at Honolulu, just in time for them to see the ship they were to take for Oregon setting its sails. That meant the couple had a wait of three months until another ship arrived for them to book passage to Oregon. The news of the Whitman massacre had reached the Islands, and an attempt was made to keep the Atkinsons from going on to the coast. They were told to stay, that there was missionary work right there in the Islands. Atkinson's answer was characteristic of his determination: "I am destined to Oregon, and to Oregon I must go."[5]

The Atkinsons left the Islands on May 23, and on June 13 they crossed the Columbia River bar—the end of a 20,000-mile wedding trip for the couple. The last stretch of the journey up the Columbia to Oregon City (formerly Wallamut Falls) proved to be the most frustrating part of the long journey. A crew of Indians, piloted by a Scotsman, manned their boat, and delays were encountered because the crew became too tired to go on and needed rest. This final delay, though necessary, was faced with the Atkinsons' destination almost in sight.

Oregon City had been made the capital of Oregon, and boasted a population of 500 people. Many of the residents were missionaries and settlers who had relocated following the Whitman massacre.

Deacon Hatch, of the Congregational group of three who had begun a church in 1844 under Harvey Clark's leadership, met the Atkinsons and invited them to stay at the Hatch home until a location could be found for them. Hatch explained that there were only ten or twelve members, and Clark preached only twice a month, but with a fulltime minister now there were many who would swell the membership.

The following Sunday, George Atkinson preached at both morning and evening services in the home of Deacon Hatch. Mr. Atkinson talked to Mr. Hatch about the responsibility he had been charged with to found an acad-

---

4   Atkinson, George H.: Journal.
5   *Ibid.*

emy in Oregon. Straightaway, Peter Hatch related to him the developments taking place on the West Plain. He then suggested that he and Atkinson should take horses and ride over to meet Clark right away.

On the West Plain, the grounds had been prepared for the camp meeting and hogs had been butchered for food. On June 28, Alvin Smith noted, "moved my family to the camp ground and tended the meeting."

That same morning, June 28, Hatch saddled the horses for the pair to begin their ride. George Atkinson described his first impression of the country:

> We arose early. At 7 o.c. after breakfast and worship. we left our wives. John Jewett accompanied us. We forded the river. Passed through the town.... We crossed in the ferry boat of Mr. Moore.... We rode over a rolling country of spare woods, mostly fir, red, yellow and white. We rode 18 miles, passed one or two farms in the low level spots. We then came upon the first of the Tualatin plains. It is a prarie [sic] of about one mile square. We saw two large fields of wheat of 50 or 60 acres. A log house with cattle and horses were around. We passed a small portion of woods and came to another such prarie. We passed again through a larger piece of woods and came to a larger prarie of 5 to 10 miles extent. Passed farms, log houses, a garden with apple and peach trees laden with fruit.... We rode...to Bro. Griffin's house.... I had become very much wearied and my horse had nearly given out.... After an hour's rest we turned toward the S.W. along the border of the prarie and rode through woods and upon an elevated prarie which presented an inclined plane surrounded with woods. 3 or 4 miles across it we saw Bro. Nailors [sic] house. In another direction Bro. Clarks. We arrived there about 7 o.c.[6]

They found that Clark was not yet home from the camp meeting. Emeline Clark met them holding her baby, James, in her arms, and with her little daughter, Satira Emeline. She invited the men to come in. Atkinson continues:

> I was glad to lie down. Mr. C. has a good claim. He keeps a few cattle and raises a few oats, and has a good garden. He built his house of logs, and made most of his own furniture. He lives very economically.

---

6   *Ibid.*

Clark came in at dusk with several ministers, and after greetings were exchanged, the others were sent to neighbors to spend the night. John Jewett and George Atkinson stayed with the Clarks, and, as would be expected, Bro. Clark and Atkinson "conversed until after midnight." As the diary details, Clark related his experiences since coming west, and about the newly started orphan school and its program that "invites district scholars whose parents pay tuition," Atkinson stated. "It is a good site and it may grow to some importance. Rev. Mr. Thompson is to instruct this term."

It is interesting to read Atkinson's own journal at this point, keeping in mind that this data was sent east to the Home Missionary Society on July 11, 1848. This is probably the most complete report to have reached their desks up to this time.

> One week I spent at a camp meeting under the direction of Brother Clark, a Congregational minister. He had had meetings for several years – Methodists, Baptists, Cumberland Presbyterians, Old and New Presbyterians were there, and all preached in turn. We have no rain this season, and it is very comfortable camping in the oak grove. There is a reason for camp meetings in the want of meeting houses. Brother Clark has only a small log house. Much truth was preached, and apparently with good results. Brother Clark is but poorly supported by his people, yet he lives among them in the most economical way, and trusts that bye and bye they will increase in wealth and numbers.... Last spring he commenced an orphan school, designed at first for children whose parents died on the journey, yet it received all and is the only school in the vicinity.... An aged lady gives her time to them. The location is good for an academy.

The fact that in this week so much information had been shared between Clark and Atkinson suggests that they spent much time together between the sessions of the camp meeting itself. Atkinson's journal continues:

> Brother Griffin, another Congregational minister came out on a similar errand. He is also on the Tualatin Plains, but he has no church now.

> On Sabbath, July 2nd, sacrament was administered on camp ground to people of different names, but of the same spirit, I trust. I assisted Mr. Clark and administered the ordinance of baptism to several children, one of these of an Indian mother, who that day united with the church after having given evidence of piety for two years. One or more females are members of his church.

The camp meeting was over at the end of the Sunday session recorded and the settlers began their exodus until the next gathering was called. But George Atkinson's fertile mind was at work and he urged further action while the ministers were together.

The next day, Monday, July 3, Mr. Atkinson writes:

> We left the plain, or Brother Clark's at two o'clock P.M. on Monday. We met, however, on the camp ground, and formed the Oregon Tract Society, auxiliary to the American Tract Society, and four of us took means to form a Territorial Association of Ministers and Churches.

Harvey Clark was overjoyed at the arrival of a man with the competence that George Atkinson possessed. He was also relieved to turn over the Oregon City church responsibility to the new co-worker, so it might have a greater ministry than he had been able to give. Clark had been appointed by Dr. Badger in 1845 as the general agent of the American Missionary Society for Oregon at an annual salary of $600. Now Clark could write to Badger from his heart, "You can hardly conceive the joy we felt when Bros Atkinson and Lyman came to our aid."[7]

Atkinson decided to make an exploration of the Willamette Valley for his own education, and chose Bro. Walker and John Gulick to go with him on July 12. Their first stop was at Harvey Clark's, where they found "several Brethern" waiting for them, and "we formed ourselves into a religious Association naming it the Oregon Association of the Congregational and Presbyterian Brethren." Churches would be admitted as they accepted the Articles, and would be entitled to one delegate from each church. Officers were chosen and the meeting adjourned until "the 20th of September next when the Association will meet at this place."[8]

At the September meeting of the newly formed Association, it was recorded:

---

7   Clark, Harvey: Report in Home Mission Files, Chicago Theological Seminary.

8   Eells, Rev. Myron, History of the Congregational Association of Oregon and Washington Territory, 1848-1880.

Rev. Messrs. Walker, Spalding, Thompson, Clark and Atkinson met at the house of Bro Harvey Clark at the Tualatin Plains. Articles of an Association for the Congregational and Presbyterian brethren were submitted to them.[9]

A constitution and bylaws were adopted and meetings were held every year, except 1852, in Oregon City or Tualatin Plains. Mrs. Atkinson, clarifying material in her husband's journal, made this additional note:

> The Association embraced several Congregational ministers, and one Old School Presbyterian, viz. a Rev. Mr. Thompson of Clatsop Plains, where, I think he had a church. This, if I'm not mistaken, was the only church and only minister of that order. Rev. Mr. Thompson soon withdrew from our association.

Bro. Griffin refused to come to the meetings or to join the Association, professing that he was a member of the Lorain Association in Ohio. Walker and Spalding, missionaries with Dr. Whitman, now lived on the West Plain. In 1859, Henry Spalding, the last of the Presbyterian ministers, withdrew and the name became "The Congregational Association of Oregon."[10]

In those days, the roads were so bad and the members so scattered that the attendance at Association meetings was small. In November 1851, for instance, only four persons attended, but the session lasted three days. This small attendance was not for lack of interest, but a factor of weather and distance.

The second Association meeting laid the groundwork for the future. It was held in Oregon City, on September 21, 1848, while the weather was good and the roads passable. It was well planned, thanks to Atkinson's mind for detail. A page from the Record Book of the Trustees of the Tualatin Academy follows:

> At a meeting of the Association of Congregational and Presbyterian brethren at Oregon City, Sept. 21st, 1848, it was resolved that it is expedient to found an Academy under its patronage.
>
> On discussion it was thought that the Tualatin Plains is the most favorable

---

9   *Ibid.*
10   *Ibid.*

location.

> After continued discussion it was resolved that we will appoint Trustees, who shall locate an Academy, become incorporated, and attend to its interests.[11]

Nine trustees were named for the task ahead: "Rev. Harvey Clark, Rev. George Atkinson, Mr. Peter H. Hatch, Esq., Mr. Hiram Clark, Esq., Rev. Lewis Thompson, Mr. William H. Gray, Esq., Mr. Alvin T. Smith, Esq., Mr. James Moore, Esq., and Mr. O. [Osborne] Russell, Esq."

Rev. Harvey Clark was appointed President of the Board of Trustees, and Rev. George H. Atkinson was named Secretary. While the other trustees have appeared by name in earlier chapters, it is interesting to get better acquainted with them.

Peter Hatch was a contractor in Oregon City and an original member of the Congregational Church that Clark had started. Hiram Clark was also an Oregon City resident, conducting a mercantile business with George Abernethy, who had been the provisional governor. Hiram Clark had brought with him to Oregon two slaves, Adoniram and Jennie Clark. Once there, he decided to free his slaves, allowing Adoniram's work to pay for his freedom and that of his wife. He also built a boat and called it the "Jennie Clark."

Rev. Lewis Thompson was a Presbyterian minister who was active in the Clark camp meetings and in the temperance movement. William Gray, who came as a mechanic with Dr. Whitman in 1838, and later at Lee's Oregon Institute, was concerned about education in the settlements. Some years later, Gray also wrote a *History of Oregon*, in which he said, "Harvey Clark was the getter-up of Pacific University." Alvin Smith we have already seen in action, and it was fitting that he should share in this phase of education. James Moore was another layman who had come west in the 1840 migration with the Clark party and had served with Gray in provisional government committees. And, Osborne Russell, for long years a trapper, was a well-educated man who later wrote *The Annals of a Trapper*.

These trustees were sound, intelligent men committed to the best for education and the Oregon Territory. A later meeting of the trustees named Alvin Smith treasurer and Hiram Clark auditor.[12]

---

11   Record Book of Trustees of Tualatin Academy, Pacific University.

12   Scott, Harvey W., *The Oregon Country* and other sources.

On September 25, the Trustees held another meeting in the office of Hiram Clark at Oregon City and it was

> Resolved that Messrs Harvey Clark and A.T. Smith solicit subscriptions for the Academy in Tualatin county, and Messrs Hiram Clark and G.H.
> Atkinson solicit them in Clackamas.[13]

That same month, Mr. L.C.D. Latourette arrived in Oregon, and in October Clark and Atkinson engaged him to teach at their school. On November 30, a third meeting of the newly created Board of Trustees was held in Oregon City and

> It was unanimously resolved that the Academy be located at the Tualatin Plains, near the Orphan Asylum.

> The Trustees resolved to form a constitution. Rev. G.H. Atkinson and Rev.
> H. Clark were appointed to draft it.[14]

They also discussed a building, which should measure "40 by 30, two stories high," and the cost of erecting such a building.

At a meeting on December 1, 1848, the report gave the estimated cost of such a building as $1,000, and it was "resolved to have a frame building." The new constitution was adopted at the same meeting, and the name "Tualatin Academy" was used for the first time.

The first definite steps toward the planned construction were made at the meeting in Tualatin Plains 11 days later:

> The Trustees resolved themselves into a committee of the whole, and discussed the main question, whether it be expedient to go on with the Academy now. It was finally resolved, that our Agent employ a man to put up a frame, and enclose it if the funds subscribed and in prospect be made available.[15]

---

13   Record Book of Trustees.
14   *Ibid.*
15   *Ibid.*

The term "agent" they used refers to article 7 of the constitution: "The Trustees shall have power to employ one of their Board as an Agent to transact their business." The Agent named was Rev. Harvey Clark.

A day later, on December 12 at 8 a.m., the site was reported on verbally, rather than appearing as a land survey. The Record Book states:

> Trustees met. Called to order by the President [H. Clark]. Examined the Ground on which to locate. Set the stakes, commencing on the east line, near the N.E. corner of the church lot. Rev. Clark promises to give ten acres of his claim to the Academy.

Thus an Academy was born before the close of 1848, and the cherished dream of Harvey Clark became a reality. Though the building would not be erected for some time, the stakes of the Academy grounds were placed on that day.

In the meantime, something unexpected had happened a thousand miles to the south, which had repercussions in the Tualatin Plain. Gold had been discovered in California in the summer of 1848. It became an obsession that reached up to touch the settlers in Oregon. As George Atkinson reported to his uncle in the East, the event left the country in an unsettled state:

> You, in the midst of Eastern excitement, the last echoes of which have come to our ears, have doubtless heard fully of our exciting themes. It is indeed true that the most remarkable gold mines were discovered last summer in California. Thither the people from the coast, North and South, from the Islands and from the Interior have been constantly going since. Some of our citizens have returned with $500, $1000, and even $3000. Many young men have expended it and have prepared to go again. Others are leaving. Some with families, some without. We shall be almost without fellow citizens. Some danger is apprehended from the Indians. We have heard that a Governor is on his way with troops but he has not arrived....
>
> I have been preaching here for six months, with some apparently good effect.[16]

With the advent of the new year, 1849, Harvey Clark continued to see about a building by gathering data for a report at the next Trustees meeting. He

---

16   Huntington Library.

contacted a Portland man named Morrison, a Scotsman by birth who had come west in 1842. Morrison had set up a lumber and flour depot at the foot of Morrison Street, named for him. He also built the first frame house in Portland and seemed interested in the Academy project.

The Trustees of the Academy met at Harvey Clark's home in February 1849 to receive a report of the plans that Morrison was to have prepared. But Morrison did not appear as promised, with or without his plans; he had gone off to California without leaving any figures. However, the Trustees reported, "Mr. Eells would offer some plans for a building. Mr. E. being present gave a description of a building and rooms."[17]

Mr. Eells was the Rev. Cushing Eells who had come west as a missionary in 1838 and been evacuated with others to Oregon City after the Whitman massacre. Perhaps Clark and Atkinson had learned that Morrison would not appear and Cushing Eells had offered to help. Certainly, Eells had come to the meeting prepared to make a report to the Trustees.

The meeting continued on February 28, but there were still many decisions to make—the question of Latourette, the teacher, and erecting a house for him, and receiving the Asylum—and the meeting was carried over to the following day. On March 1, many of these agenda items were brought to a conclusion:

1. It was resolved to accept the Orphan Asylum for a boarding House for the School, from Rev. H. Clark, the Agent for the Asylum and to become responsible to the donors of the Asylum for $30., should they call for it.

2. It was resolved to erect a log house 32 x 22, outside, and finish it, if possible, expending the sum subscribed, $250. It is to be erected near the Asylum.

3. It was resolved that the Agent expend the funds subscribed in erecting said house for the teacher.

4. It was resolved that in consequence of the embarrassed state of the country, to defer for the present, building an Academy.

5. It was resolved to let the boarding house for a year to Mrs. Brown, the Trustees having the general oversight of it.

---

17   Record Book of Trustees.

6. Resolved that the tuition for the 1st term of eleven weeks, be $5.00 for the common branches, and $6.00 for the higher branches, to be paid at the middle of the term then current.

7. Resolved that the teacher's house be finished by the 1st of May.

8. Resolved that the first term commence the 1st Wednesday in April.

9. Resolved that the Rev. H. Clark be Supervisor of the Boarding House.

10. Resolved that the Supervisor of the Boarding House provide wood for the school at the expense of the Trustees.

11. Resolved that Messrs Smith, Harvey Clark and Eells, if here, locate the teacher's house.

The Trustees engaged Rev. C. Eells as teacher and Principal of the School for the next term and onwards, providence permitting, and insured him 30 scholars at $5.00 per term.

It would appear that nothing had been left to chance in building a sure foundation for the future. In his diary, Alvin Smith records his part in the proceedings:

Mar 1 tended a meeting of the trustees of the Academy & agreed to furnish
        flour meat & potatoes for the boarding school for 3 months my
        donation to the boarding house and children there - Butts, Stokes,
        Stephens, Jones & Terwilligers Children 16 in number.

Smith names the 16 children enrolled in the boarding house, which would leave 14 to be gleaned from the neighboring community as day students if Cushing Eells was to have the 30 students assured him by the Trustees.

One of the boys enrolled was Myron Eells, son of Cushing Eells, and some years later he described the school room:

The first one used after the trustees took charge of the school was the old log
building which was put up for a church. It was about twenty by thirty feet
and twelve feet high, with puncheon seats and desks. A log was split in two,
the split side was hewed as smoothly as possible, one half with pins for legs

was used for a seat, and the other half was fastened to the wall for a desk. The older scholars had these, and when they wished could face the desk and wall and write, or if they wished could turn around and have the desk for a back. But the smaller scholars, who were not large enough to write, had a bench near the middle of the floor, with no desk, and no chance to rest their backs.

The floor also consisted of puncheons, but in the course of time, as they lay very near the ground, the edges rotted and fell away, much as they do now on some very rough bridges on the frontiers, and the writer remembers very well that one crack was so large that he put his small bare foot through it.

The building had a batten door, and the logs were cut away so as to receive a few panes of glass for windows, a half window on a side. This was the birthplace of the school which is now Pacific University.[18]

Latourette, engaged in October 1848 by Messrs. Clark and Atkinson to teach school, severed his connection with the school in March of the following year. He, too, was headed for the gold fields. Fortunately, Cushing Eells was available and willing to become Latourette's successor.

Alvin Smith had it impressed on him that he, Clark and Eells were to locate the teacher's house and have it built by May 1, so he hired help. On March 30, he "paid Clark Pringle $21.25 for his work on the Academy." Clark Pringle was Mrs. Brown's grandson.

The following day, Smith "went to Mr. Knightons and to the saw mill to see about some lumber for the Academy." A sample of the Smith diary shows his concentration on the new project:

Apr 7   halled the sills for the teachers house miller brought 24 bushels of
    wheat & left 10 at Br Clarks

Apr 18 worked on the Academy building [the teacher's house]

Apr 19 got my grist & took some flour & potatoes to the boarding house

May 24 went to the boarding house with some flour

---

18   Eells, Myron, son of Cushing Eells, missionary; manuscript in Pacific University.

> May 29 went to the falls with a grist & to the saw mill & brought away the balance of my lumber that I had bought of Mr Wood & paid Mr Eells the Tuition of Mr Stephens Child

In addition to his labors on the new academy, Smith still found time to "help Mr. Clark kill a beef," "cradle oats for Mr. Clark," attend trustee meetings and finish laying the floors in the meeting house. Though the church had been used for preaching and for classes, certain details in finishing it still had to be completed.

In like manner, as supervisor of the boarding house, Clark was jotting instructions for his fellow trustee, Alvin Smith:

> Brother Smith will you let me have one bushel of white wheat, if not white red, we wish it to boil mostly for Mrs. Brown, and much obliged
>
> H. Clark[19]

The new Governor, Joseph Lane, who had been appointed by the U.S. Government in 1848, at last arrived from the East in 1849. At the same time, George Atkinson was moving ahead with his long-range plan for education. Atkinson brought out his ideas on the public education that was needed as the.west became more populated. While only private schools were available at that time, plans must be made ahead of time to give free schools to every community, he said. On June 28, 1849, an important step was taken by the Academy's trustees as they "Resolved to obtain an Act of Incorporation from the present legislature."[20]

This was a great occasion for George Atkinson, and he hastened to share his joy with his relatives in the East:

> I am now with others endeavoring to establish an Academy. Indeed we have been for the last nine months. We have a teacher, Rev. C. Eells. He is an excellent teacher. He has now 58 scholars mostly small [young]. We have put him in a log house costing about six hundred dollars. Labor is from 1 to 5 dollars per day. We have sold him the house and next year we hope to erect an Academy building. He now teaches in a log church. We need a female

---

19   Papers in Pacific University Archives.
20   Record Book of Trustees.

assistant. Mrs. E [Eells] is not able to continue in the school. I shd rejoice to see a dozen young and educated ladies of New England here. We cd find them places in a week as teachers and pay them from 3 to 8 dollars per week, providing they would teach awhile.... We hope to establish a Free School system this year for the territory.[21]

George Atkinson lost little time in getting acquainted with Gov. Lane, and found him a willing listener to the Atkinson suggestions about free schools. In his Inaugural Address July 17, 1849, Gov. Lane made a ringing plea for education. The address mirrored Atkinson's thoughts because the speech material had been prepared by Atkinson. The legislature responded, and on September 6, 1849, it adopted the Territory's first school law.

That same month, Atkinson wrote to his uncle, Josiah Little, explaining the needs in Oregon and hoping for funds or access to them through his uncle:

We are wanting teachers.... Some object to giving us an act of Incorporation for our Academy at the Tualatin Plains. But a law like that of New York will enable us to do all we wish....

I hope you and other liberal friends of education at the East will assist us to furnish an institution with apparatus and to make funds for the teacher's support. He is now supported by the scholars and we are building by subscription. We shall hope to increase the facilities. Few of our people as yet have come to the territory.[22]

On September 3, the members of the legislature changed the county's name from Tualatin to Washington County. One of the legislators said he just could not say Tualatin or spell it because there were too many pronunciations. All agreed, and it became Washington, honoring the first President.

The urgency to establish an incorporated academy came before there were enough settlers to carry the costs, as Atkinson had noted, and the legislature was too young to take up the establishment of laws governing education. But, Atkinson, Clark and the Trustees were determined. The Act of Incorporation was granted to them on September 26th. Since it was the

---

21   Huntington Library.
22   *Ibid.*

first charter to be granted to an educational institution in the Oregon Territory, it is reproduced here:

An Act to Establish a Seminary In
Washington County

Sec. 1 Be it enacted by the Legislative Assembly of the territory of Oregon, that there shall be established for the instruction of persons of both sexes in science and literature to be called the "Tualatin Academy", and that George H. Atkinson, Harvey Clark, James Moore, Peter H. Hatch, Lewis Thompson, William H. Gray, Hiram Clark, A.T. Smith and J.Q. Thornton and their successors are hereby declared to be a body politic and corporate in law by the name and style as "The President and Trustees of the Tualatin Academy."[23]

Other sections followed, clarifying details and stipulating procedures that usually follow such acts.

In his years on the West Plain, Clark had added to his claim, acquired from Orus Brown, another parcel of land which had belonged to a Solomon Emerick. Emerick had sold his claim to a man named Carey for a "merchandise order on the Hudson's Bay Company for six dollars," and Clark purchased it from Mr. Carey. This parcel adjoined the north line of Clark's original property and made up the northern section of the campus which became Pacific University.[24]

On December 1, Atkinson again pressured his uncle, Josiah Little:

The Academy of which I have written you, that we hoped to establish, is in operation. We have now only log buildings. There are two departments. Rev. C. Eells is the principal. This year we have a man in the primary department. Usually we have a lady. We hope to have a Female Teacher from the east who can instruct in Music and some of the branches of less intrinsic value but of much more importance in keeping children from the papists. We obtained an act of Incorporation at the Legislature by which we are allowed to extend the Academy to the privileges of a college. Our great hope is to be

---

23   Record Book of Trustees.
24   Carey, Charles.

successful in this enterprise. We proposed erecting a building 30 by 60, two stories in height the coming year but it may not be accomplished so early.[25]

Atkinson's fear of the "papists" was not as keen as the Catholic concern about the Protestants, for in several cases, the priest to the south came into Washington County and forced Catholic families to resettle within his church's territory. There was apparently a fear on both sides of losing souls.

Atkinson in his letter to his uncle did not forget the uppermost thing in his mind—money. His letter continues in that vein:

> We expect some donations from the Mon. concert at the Sandwich Islands. We have some funds on hand and a few hundred dollars pledged, but lumber and labor are very high. We expect some means by a sale of lots donated in a land claim to us. We are in want of all kinds of School apparatus except books; of these I have about $100 worth which have just arrived from New York. Should you think favorably of our project we hope you will render us whatever aid may be consistent with your numerous calls.

Friends in the Islands who remembered the winter the Atkinsons spent with them on their way to Oregon were helpful in setting up these Monday Concerts for Tualatin Academy. Rev. S. Damon, a publisher of *The Friend*, a paper distributed in the Islands, had recently paid a visit to the school. He had come to visit Mrs. Eells, since both of them had originally come from Holden, Massachusetts. While at the Plain, he had become much interested in this school of which Eells was the Principal, and upon his return to the Islands, he wrote an article about the founding of Tualatin Academy, and closed by saying:

> I resolved upon my return to the Islands to present the claims of Tualatin Academy. There I fancied I saw the foundations being laid of an institution, which might in due time vie with the colleges and Universities on the shores of the Atlantic.[26]

---

25   Huntington Library.
26   Eells, Myron: manuscript.

Damon's writing and the friendships made by the Atkinsons, in addition to the Eells' contact from Holden, brought financial advantages to the young academy.

As the year 1849 came to a close, all were willing to agree that the beginnings had been difficult. There were still the scarcity of population, the upsetting influence of the California Gold Rush, the stumbling blocks that settlers in the young territory faced to establish a working government and the difficulty of trying to recreate a life they remembered from the East.

One incident offers a cameo picture of this period. We know of Atkinson's many trips by horseback through the canyon between Oregon City and Tualatin Plain. (His fellow Trustee, Peter Hatch, was a small, bent man and usually walked.) On one occasion, a man berated Atkinson for riding a horse when he was asking others to sacrifice and donate money to the Academy. Straightaway, Atkinson sold the horse and proceeded to walk the remaining distance. He was an idealist, so the story may have been true. We can be equally sure that he later bought another horse as a necessity in order to complete his rounds of the territory.

But this is a fitting anecdote to reflect the idealism and hopes—and the poverty and hardship—that these people carried at the end of that decade.

Chapter 8
The Growing Establishment: 1850-1852

It became apparent by the start of the new decade that a certain settling in was beginning to take place. Certainly, there was a greater sense of domesticity among the settlers than seen in the preceding decade, although not all signs were positive.

For example, in 1850 the residents in this new country had particular difficulties trying to balance their household budgets. George Atkinson reported the conditions to his cousin, Josiah Hale, in the East:

> Prices increase so rapidly that it is [only] with greatest care that we can live within our means. I work up my own wood. It wd cost $18 to $20 per cord to buy it.... Butter has risen from 30 cents to $1.25 per lb within six months. Eggs are $1.00 per doz (but we sell instead of buy). Potatoes are from $3 to $7 per bushel.[1]

In spite of these costs, Mr. Atkinson was still able to continue his contributions to his missionary interests. Upon moving to Oregon City, one of the first things he had done was to plant two apple trees, one for Foreign missions and one for Home missions. Every year thereafter, the apples from one tree were sold to help the Foreign mission program; the apples of the other tree brought money for the Home mission program of his church or denomination.

And there was fruitfulness of another kind. Alvin Smith noted on February 2 that "Mrs. Smith helped bring the Clark son into the world." This was William, the third child in the Clark family. Though Emeline Clark's

---

1   Huntington Library.

life at this time was largely spent in raising her family, we can be sure that she rejoiced with her husband in the growth of the dream she and Harvey had nurtured for ten years.[2]

In the spring, the Portland contractor Mr. Morrison returned from the gold fields after an absence of two years, and worked on the long-promised plans for the Academy building. He presented a plan to the Trustees on April 16, 1850, and they "Resolved to locate the building in the morning."

Another important resolution made that day was to ask Samuel Thurston to present the interests of the Academy to Congress and request 640 acres of land. He was also asked to present Clark's claim, as missionary, for an additional 640 acres. This land was requested under the Donation Land Claim Act passed in 1850, which would give 320 acres to a single person and 640 acres to a married couple who should settle in the territory before December 1, 1850. Clark had already staked out his claim of 640 acres, according to the Provisional Government, but the additional Academy request was not accepted in Washington.

On the second day of the Trustee's meeting, the record reports:

> The Trustees visited the grounds near Rev. H. Clark's church to locate the building. They decided that it shall be from the East and shall stand on the division line between the Clark and Stokes claims. Six rods from and parallel with Washington street having Main street immediately in the rear at a right angle with Washington street.[3]

In May, a scroll with the word "seal" inserted was adopted as a seal of the corporation. At the same time, on May 1, "it was resolved to receive the History of Harvard University." This meant a library, and Rev. Cushing Eells was elected Librarian of the institution.

Orders were given at the same time to "erect, inclose, or cover the building, exclusive of the windows, according to the Morrison Plan."[4] With Harvey Clark serving as agent as well as president of the Board of Trustees, the responsibility fell on his shoulders to ensure that the job was completed.

---

2   Scott, Harvey W., vol. II.
3   Record Book of Trustees.
4   *Ibid.*

Much work had gone into the physical labor preparatory to erecting the new building. The spring had seen steady activity as the men hewed and hauled timbers, while other men were busy framing them together.

It was the period of "bee raisings," in which neighbors helped neighbors because the raising of a structure required many men of muscle. But it was also a time for neighborly fun as well. Up until this time, earlier buildings had been made of logs; this was to be a frame structure, made of hand-hewn posts and beams 10 inches square. Notices had gone out by word of mouth to people in the area, with an invitation to come and help on the stated date.

Squire Tuttle was adept at such raisings and had supervised the work of assembling the materials so they would be ready for the big day of the actual raising. Tuttle's title "squire" was an honorary one, given to anyone who was older, trained in his profession and a respected personage in the community. And Tuttle was all of those things. He must have been excited with the raising, for he was the man responsible for orchestrating its completion. He was glad to see a large number of men and their families come in their cloth-covered ox wagons and horse-drawn carts, ready for camping until the job was done. Indeed, the construction required two days to complete. The landscape under the oak trees looked much like the camp meetings of the period, and all were happy to enjoy the change from ordinary home duties.

Mrs. Elkanah Walker was instrumental in organizing the Maternal Society, both in Oregon City and West Tualatin Plain. So it was natural that she would be one of the group of women who busied themselves feeding the people who came on that summer day to help raise the Academy building. Her diary records the day:

> July 9, 1850 – Helped prepare the dinner for raising the Academy. Quite a number of the ladies met and we had a social time.[5]

Marcus Walker, Elkanah's son, was there. He was a small boy then, but was impressed enough to recall the occasion on May 25, 1895, in the *San Francisco Pacific*:

> Tables were set in the old log building, partly church, which has passed into history as the birthplace of Tualatin Academy and Pacific University, where bountiful dinners were provided by the women for the men at work, this

---

5   Drury, Clifford, *Elkanah and Mary Walker.*

department being under the energetic oversight of "Grandma" [Tabitha] Brown, with her stern face and dignified bearing, but we knew that behind them lay the kindest heart that ever befriended an orphan.[6]

Marcus Walker continued to describe the drama surrounding the actual raising of the structure:

> When all was ready, and Squire Tuttle took his stand in some prominent position, and gave the word, "He, oh, heave" and bent after bent slowly rose to place, it seemed to me that an event was transpiring grander than anything else I could compare with it.

The men stationed at specific locations held the frames until they were well-anchored in place and the Squire gave his appreciative nod. And, with the covering of the structure against the weather, there stood the frame of the Academy and completion of the raising.

Marcus Walker's article goes on to explain details of the next steps required to finish the building:

> But money was scarce in those days, and houses were not built in a hurry, and so a winter and a second summer passed away before even one room was ready. It was, if I rightly recall it, a frosty morning in October 1851, when twenty-five or thirty of us gathered in the lower north room and school began, with Mr. J.M. Keeler on the platform. We could not boast even one professor that day.

The building that saw so many hands joined in common enterprise in 1850 and '51 stands today as Old College Hall, one of the oldest educational buildings west of the Mississippi River. Its original location (for it has been moved several times) was on the present site of Marsh Hall, facing east. Of course, it was discouraging in 1850 to have completed raising of the frame and to not be able to complete the building, but no one would make a bid to finish construction—including outside doors made by hand. Lumber was worth twenty or thirty dollars at the mill, forty or sixty dollars delivered.

---

6   Walker, Marcus, the *San Francisco Pacific*, May 25, 1895. As a newspaperman, Marcus Walker occasionally wrote of his earlier experiences.

Carpenters charged from eight to ten dollars per day.[7] But Clark was finally able to finish one room, and the rest of the building was boarded up until such time as it could also be finished. In spite of this economic challenge being slowly overcome, everyone did not view the building as positively as Clark and his associates. Mary (Mrs. Elkanah) Walker probably expressed the sentiment of many people when she wrote in her diary on Sept. 11, 1851:

> Went inside the Academy for the first time. A splendid monument to the folly of somebody. Wonder who will live to see it completed and filled with students.[8]

While it did look like folly without the money at hand to complete the work, Mrs. Walker was interested and concerned. She sold her gold watch valued at $200 to Deacon Naylor and paid Squire Tuttle what was due him.[9]

But this bit of information does not mean that there were no other problems. The Trustees faced a number of problems throughout the remainder of 1850 while the building was still an unfinished shell.

There were endless meetings of the trustees, the details of which Atkinson chronicled:

> Many a trip was made from Oregon City and Portland and Salem to Forest Grove, or vice versa, on horseback or in lumber wagon, or on foot, in summer heat or winter storms and mud to study and solve the oft repeated questions of the academy and the college, the instructors and the books, their costs and funds to pay them.

> At one time, as we seemed ready to fall apart, and give up the enterprise. Mrs. Brown, Mrs. Clark, and Mrs. A.T. Smith, who overheard our remarks through the almost open ceiling of the log house, came to the door, and begged us to hold on and go forward, while they also joined in prayer by themselves, on our behalf, and on behalf of the cause.[10]

---

7   Walker, June: Manuscript of her report for Pacific Charter Day program, January 1925.

8   Walker, Mary: diary entry September 11, 1851.

9   Walker, June: Pacific Charter Day.

10   Atkinson, George H.

The trials of the school were enough to tax a man's spirit. In the fall of 1850, Alvin Smith decided that even if Clark had been called to be their minister for another year, the reverend should be "stated supply"—a temporary status. Once before, Smith had talked to Alanson Hinman about Clark because the minister had missed preaching on several Sundays. This time, Smith was more determined, feeling that Clark was involved in too many other endeavors.

Clark asked Smith his reasons for calling him a "stated supply." Smith's answer: "I told him of one thing because of his stopping preaching last winter." The pull between duties in a church and a school was apparent, yet both were of great importance. Granted that Clark was ill for several weeks during the bad weather, still Smith believed the church came first and was the more important of his duties.

Added to Clark's problems with Smith over church duties, Cushing Eells presented his resignation. After having taught for a year and a half, Eells announced he could not and would not teach where the students used tobacco. Furthermore, he had not approved of the Academy building designed by Morrison and so recently built.

This resignation led to a resolution by the Trustees that "no scholar should be continued in the school who used tobacco in or about the school house, or while under the care and control of the Teacher or Principal."[11]

There was also a matter of broader concern to the Trustees, and that focused on planning for a town and bringing settlers into the college community. So far, land claims made up the composition of this part of West Plain. The southern area—where the Smith, Clark, Naylor and Hinman claims were located—was called "Yankee Town," for the four families of Yankee background who lived there. Alvin Smith lived in one log house in this area and used a second log building, in the present-day Carnation Mill area, for a post office. Since mail came only once a week, settlers made few trips to the post office. As the settlement grew, however, Mrs. Smith was certified as the assistant postmistress to her husband.

North of the post office, the Clark claim proceeded to the swale, a low-lying wet and boggy area that carried enough water seasonally that a half-log bridge with side rails had been built. Much later, the water was directed underground, which ended the need for a bridge crossing. Above this swale, the land became a pleasant hill, with a beautiful setting of oak and fir trees.

11   Trustees Report, G. Atkinson, secretary.

Now, the Trustees were faced with finding a name for the town and laying out lots which would be sold for the benefit of the new Academy.

The town was laid out to the following measurements: Regular blocks were six chains plus 10 links square. A regular street is one chain wide, which according to the dictionary is 100 links, or 66 feet. A regular block, then, was 402-3/5 feet square; a regular street was 66 feet wide.

Atkinson's description of how the town was laid out provides a picture of the present town's beginnings:

> The gift of two hundred acres by Rev. H. Clark at first became the sure basis for the enterprise. Further acreage of Mr. Clark's claim were given to the school for a town. The village was plotted in four acre blocks including streets, giving ample space for residence and campus. The additional gifts of Rev. E. Walker and by Deacon T. Naylor extended the village limits to valuable and attractive proportions.... The gifts of Messrs Buxton, Catching and others at a later date confirmed the permanence of the location.
>
> The original condition, that the sale of intoxicating drinks is forbidden in the deed of the property and of every lot sold, on penalty of forfeit of title, has added to the moral protection of the youth gathered there, and to the families as well.[12]

While the lots were plotted and ready to market, at least on paper, a town name still had to be found for properly recording the sales. George Atkinson suggested the name Vernon. He knew of a town in the East by that name and liked the sound of it. There was no response from the Trustees, so it was decided to wait until the next day for a decision. In the meantime, they instructed the Agent, Clark, to complete enclosing the new building and finish one room.

The next day, January 10, the Trustees voted to employ a male teacher and a female "if one comes," and that a Principal be hired at "a salary not to exceed seven hundred dollars a year."

> Then it was remarked that towns, or plots laid out as towns, for the sale of lots must be recorded, under a heavy penalty.
>
> Moved by Mr. Atkinson and seconded to call the town Vernon. Rejected.

---

12 Record Book of Trustees.

Moved by Mr. Thornton and seconded that the name of the town be Forest Grove. Passed.

The name Forest Grove is credited to Mrs. Thornton. Her husband said on his return from the first meeting of the Trustees that they must have a name. She said that she had been so impressed by the grove of oaks and the forest of firs side by side, why not call the place where the two stands of trees came together Forest Grove? The meeting continued with details of the new town:

Resolved to sell lots at $200. each, but that the Agent be permitted to sell at $100 if, in his judgment, it seems best to complete the seminary.

Resolved that Hiram Clark, Esq. obtain a bell at San Francisco or New York of not less than 500 lbs.[13]

The Trustees then took another step forward by deciding that it was time to advertise. Their advertising was placed on January 16, 1851, in the Oregon City *Spectator* the first newspaper in the territory. In glowing terms, the ad set out the advantages of the Academy:

Tualatin Academy

This institution is situated in the town of Forest Grove, Tualatin Plains. It is now in its infancy, yet parents and guardians desiring to send to this school may be assured not only of the healthfulness and beauty of the location, but especially that such teachers will be employed as will make the highest mental and moral improvement of the scholars, their chief subject.

A spacious and noble Academy building has been erected upon a site commanding the view of two extensive prairies with their intervening and encircling hills, and, when completed, it will furnish accommodations for both departments of the school. Forest Grove is about equidistant from the towns of St. Helens, Milton, Portland, Milwaukie, Oregon City and Lafayette.

---

13   *Ibid.*

The resolution recommending the employment of a female teacher—if one came—suggests there was a continuing quest for young women who would teach in the Oregon Territory. Women teachers were in short supply. Mrs. Clark had taught in the beginning, but now her children occupied her time, and Mrs. Eells taught one year but could not continue.

Finally, one such woman, Miss Elizabeth Miller, did answer the call in New England. The story she wrote in 1899 for her daughter details her experiences, with all the spontaneity of the days as they happened.

Miss Miller graduated in Albany, N.Y., in March 1850. She wanted to teach, but her parents insisted that she rest after her schooling. Returning home after graduation, she told her father, a minister, how much she wanted a teaching career. As she went with him on his parish rounds, she learned he had some ideas too, one of which was to go to Oregon. His Synod suggested he might be sent out to start a mission there.

Then Elizabeth Miller read of the call for teachers, an appeal from the citizens of Oregon, begging the National Board of Popular Education to send teachers west. With her parents' permission, she went to Hartford, Conn., to apply in person. She carried a letter from her pastor, who was her father, and one from a person whom the Board might use as a reference to her teaching ability. Of the group of young women applying for positions, Miss Miller was the only one who desired to go to Oregon; the others wanted positions in the Mississippi Valley, not so far from home.

After the acceptance, she spent the winter in preparation for her journey west, with a brief time at the Troy Seminary spent in study. When the time of departure arrived, the only drawback was that her parents could not join her. They would be going to Oregon, but there were no berths available for them on the ship. Elizabeth, a young woman of twenty, had only her brother, Frank, four years her junior, for company. She was in safe hands, however, for she and other teachers were under the care of Samuel Thurston, an Oregonian and Representative in Congress.

This trip was very different from that of Harvey Clark, who crossed overland, or George Atkinson, who went by sea around Cape Horn, for these passengers traveled on land across the Isthmus of Panama. Their discomfort on this portage through the jungle was compounded by unsafe drinking water and the sometimes dangerous riding by muleback.

With the crossing completed, the travelers arrived at the port of Old Panama, where Thurston became very ill. He died before the party reached Acapulco. All of the travelers grieved for the kind man's death, but young Elizabeth felt a real hardship: Thurston had been carrying her purse for security, and when he died it was sealed with his personal possessions. As a result, she had to proceed north without any money for the rest of the trip.

The ship *California* carried the party up the West Coast to Astoria, where the party boarded the newly built steamer, *Lot Whitcomb* for the trip up the Columbia River. To Elizabeth Miller, tired and homesick, the surroundings looked most desolate:

> There were a very few woodsmen's huts on the banks between Astoria and Vancouver; and the less said of my feelings the better.

> The Hudson Bay Company's building and stockades were then all complete and full of interest. We were soon at Portland, and walked up from the steamer's gangplank through a double line of gazers composed of the entire population of Portland. No arrival had yet taken place of so many women. The one-sided community was exceedingly interested.[14]

From Portland, a whaling boat took the party up the Willamette to Oregon City. With no purse, Miss Miller became increasingly apprehensive about her future. The boat was due to arrive at Oregon City about four in the afternoon. On approaching the Clackamas River, much later than scheduled, the boat stuck fast to a bar—perhaps because the boatmen had been drinking whisky. The passengers—cold and hungry—remained uncomfortable all night, seeing the lights of Oregon City so close but impossible to reach.

Refusing to wait for daylight, some of the men went ashore. They found a canoe on the Clackamas bank, paddled across the river through unfamiliar country and reached shore at Oregon City. There, they told of the boat stuck on the bar and broke the news of the death of Thurston, the Territory's representative.

In the morning, a rescue party brought the tired travelers to Oregon City, and Miss Miller describes her welcome:

> On the bridge a little north of the Congregational Church we met Dr., then Mr. Atkinson. He was a fine looking man, really quite young, he was thirty-two.... He was from Vermont and naturally, I am sure, of a grave and serious temperament.

> Mr. Atkinson's house was a small neat building.... The exquisite neatness

---

14   Miller, Elizabeth: typed manuscript, Pacific University.

and homelikeness of everything, and a dainty dinner, which soon followed our arrival, did much to put us to peace with the world.

She met Judge Thornton in Oregon City soon after her arrival, and as a Trustee he must have been relieved to know that at last there was a woman teacher for the Academy.

During the first week in June 1851, Elizabeth Miller was taken to her new home. Deacon Naylor and Harvey Clark came from Forest Grove, and with Mrs. Thornton and Elizabeth they made their way across the hills and plains by horseback. The final leg of the trip was perhaps a rude awakening to Miss Miller, for she wrote with irony:

> Much was said about the excellence of my mount. Deacon N. had borrowed him, especially for the new teacher's use. I cannot conceive what it would have been had any common horse been put to my service. I had never ridden, except that mule ride across the Isthmus (I was large with soft muscles, all unused to such violent exercise).

The sun felt hot, the ride became more painful, but the men dared not let her dismount. Seeing Indians approaching, Elizabeth wrote with a touch of humor:

> Meeting some Indians in their usual string, instead of being afraid, I would have been glad to know they were going to shoot me.

But the Indians ignored the four on horseback.

Finally, they arrived at Forest Grove, and Miss Miller went to bed where she stayed several days, recovering from the thirty-mile horseback ride and the hardships of the trip to Oregon City. Clark was a real help. Even when Elizabeth was able to be about and felt too ill to teach her classes, she said, "Rev. Harvey Clark always kind, always sacrificing himself for others, did my work in the school room."

Knowing the young teacher was lonesome, Clark found ways to buoy her spirits, and she wrote:

> Mr. Clark, an agreeable gentleman, with a lovely wife who was always pleasant and friendly, had constituted a serene refuge. These friends would have been valued anywhere and at all times; besides, Mr. Clark had a present from Capt. Gresby, of a chaise, "One Hoss", and he had a well broken horse, which he was willing at all times, no matter how busy, to hitch up for my

use. I drove hundreds of miles over those prairies, up the mountain woodroads, often with Mrs. Clark, and sometimes with one of the older school girls.... There were few places to which the trusty steed "Lucas" could not pull the two-wheels which carried my "chariot."

On one occasion, the young teacher rode up a faint trail, hearing noises that assured her she would find people. The trail ended at a sawmill, which was apparently active, and yet no one was in sight. Suddenly, a face appeared through the bushes, and a man's voice told her this was the end of the road. She turned the chaise, and as she drove away, she was aware of heads appearing above the bushes to watch her departure. The mystery was explained by the men themselves the following Saturday. The men at the sawmill had heard about the new teacher and had cooperated to buy one new suit. The plan was that each weekend one of the men would put on the suit, go to town to trade, go to church, and of course get an introduction to the new teacher. Unfortunately, she had caught them at their worst appearance. To preserve their dignity, they had dived into the bushes at her approach. The story was repeated by the men in town with much hilarity.

Elizabeth Miller also found friendship from Mrs. Brown, sometimes in surprising ways:

> Another great comfort was the presence and counsel of Mrs. Tabitha Brown, a wise woman of about seventy-five years of age. I have never met her equal in some things.... She was of great use to me in my limited experience, always kind and helpful.

> A great trouble was my visitors. I never liked them in my teaching.... I could do better work without visitors. Often, too, I was made to feel they came wholly out of curiosity, and were altogether unsympathetic; but once it was worse than common. A young man had ridden out from Portland, and walked to the schoolroom, and came in to await the hour of dismissal, when he would make his intended call. The older girls, some of them, began to giggle and look knowing, others followed. At last I heard a whisper, "Teacher's got a beau," passing along. My cheeks burned, but not at the alleged fact. I was proof against that, but with mortification that I did not know how to meet the case.

> That evening I told Mrs. Brown. She listened to my tale of woe, as I said I must give up teaching, not having the sense of dignity enough to contend with such outbreaks of the pupils. It was useless to go on. Her bright eyes

snapped a little and she called the girls before her, and such a lecture they got. I never heard such words shot out more effectively.

She reminded them of things they had said to me, of the opportunity of school work they had so long been deprived of, and of the return they were making to me. The result was, I might have had afterwards a procession of callers without disturbing the studies of the scholars or the comfort of the teacher.

Not only does this description give a picture of a young woman adjusting to the rigors of life on the plain, but her narrative provides a fine insight into the qualities of Rev. Harvey and Emeline Clark as understanding friends, and of Mrs. Brown as a much-loved, yet stern, guide to the young in the home life of the Academy.

Another vignette of life in Forest Grove in 1851 was discovered when Elizabeth Miller attended church:

The evidence of the primitive life there was given the first Sunday of going to church. It was very hot weather; there were no fans. Each lady had a twig from the bushes bent round and both ends held in her hand, and a silk handkerchief over the whole. This custom is spoken of in W.E. Barton's "Hills of Kentucky."

The bell ordered by the Trustees in Forest Grove had been purchased and placed in the belfry of the frame school building. It was rung to call the students to classes and chapel services, and came to be known as The Chapel Bell. But it was more than the name might imply to the citizens of the community, for it was also rung to announce the approach of Indians in time of crisis, and the belfry became the watchtower in fear of an Indian attack. In this way, the watchtower became at once a symbol of the religious foundations and one of safety to the residents of the Plain.

In June 1851, a lengthy and heated Trustee meeting was held. Charges were brought by two of the Trustees, Alvin T. Smith and Peter H. Hatch, against the teacher, Rev. David R. Williams, the man who had replaced Cushing Eells. The two Trustees suggested that Rev. Williams did not enforce the prohibition against using tobacco; that he did not close his classes with a prayer, but instead closed them with a song; and that his theology was faulty, suggesting Unitarianism.

The Board heard all the evidence of these charges, and examined the teacher. They felt the evidence did not warrant dismissal, and the matter was closed with the employment of Rev. Williams for another year.[15]

This decision did not please Alvin Smith, and he stated in his diary:

> Just tended the meeting of the trustees & had an unpleasant meeting dissenting from them & resigning with one more viz P.H. Hatch.

Their resignations were accepted by the Board, but apparently the matter was still echoing at a church meeting two days later, for Smith continued:

> June 7 tended church meeting & had a very unpleasant meeting in several respects - touching the preacher (Mr. Clark) and touching giving the meeting house to David Williams as principal of the Tualatin Academy.

With these two events, Smith for the second time severed connections with Mr. Clark's projects; having resigned from the Board of Trustees, he also walked out on the church. He put the children under the care of Eells as teacher in a different school two miles north of Hillsboro, and went to other church services to underscore his disapproval.

At this time, *The Home Missionary*, a Congregational publication in the East, carried this article describing the struggling Oregon school for the enlightenment of its churches:

> Our schools are prospering. Tualatin Academy, which is more especially under the care of our denomination, is gaining in importance and in the confidence of the people. There are now 63 pupils in it – 30 in the male department under the care of Rev. D.R. Williams, and 33 in the female department under the care of Miss E. Miller, one of the teachers sent out by the Education Society.[16]

If the passions of the people surrounding church and Academy leadership seem quixotic, it is due to a continuing clash caused by the mix of cultures and personalities. Atkinson commented on these concerns over church and community when he wrote on August 8, 1851, to his cousin, Josiah Hale:

---

15   Record Book of Trustees.
16   *The Home Missionary*, November 1851.

I hardly know whether I will have twenty or forty hearers on any succeeding Sabbath. And now all who come are leaving town to take up claims. We must conform to the people in many things. They cannot or will not appreciate a style peculiarly New England. Every man believes that his own customs are best. So that every Missourian is proud of Missouri, and would reproduce many of the characteristics of its people here. A Kentuckian would do the same. So would one from North Carolina and another from New York, and another from Mass. or Vermont.[17]

That same fall, Clark began to show signs of failing health, compounded by the strains of church and Academy. Atkinson expressed the pain he shared in a letter on October 8 to his uncle, Josiah Little:

Our Academy at the Plains is prospering, but our agent, Rev. H. Clark is now laid aside from his labors by too great burdens for his strength. We trust that with rest he will recover. He may go East in the spring. We are isolated from the world at home and must have our own institutions, but to have them imposes a double work upon the ministers who see full need and who cannot rest in view of it. Other men in a new country have private interests of a foremost importance in their view. They give some money, they act as Trustees in meetings, they speak favorably, yet hardly one can spend time to carry out the endless detail of care and duty involved in the establishment of a literary Institution.[18]

Atkinson had finally faced the situation in which the Trustees were concerned about the causes they worked for, but could not give all their waking hours, day after day, to the projects that were dear to the hearts of Clark and Atkinson. By year's end, the one finished room of the Academy building was in use. The end of 1851 also saw Elizabeth Miller leave her teaching position to join her family in Albany, Oregon. She later was to marry Judge John C. Wilson and live in The Dalles.

In the spring of 1852, George Atkinson felt he must make a trip east in order to best serve the interests of the Academy in Forest Grove, and also for the Clackamas County Female Seminary that he had started. He had hoped Clark might make the trip, but the man's health had not improved,

---

17   Atkinson letters, Huntington Library.
18   *Ibid.*

and he had declined. Mrs. Atkinson noted that because of the long absence, her husband made arrangements for her and their children, Martha, aged 12, George, two and a half, and a six-month-old baby daughter. They would

> Spend the summer with the family of Rev. Mr. Clark, of Tualatin Plains. Through their kindness and self sacrifice we were cheered and encouraged during the year of absence of Mr. Atkinson.[19]

Atkinson traveled by way of Panama, using a pass given him by Capt. B. Knight, agent of the Pacific Mail Steamship Company. He arrived in New York, filled with enthusiasm for the Academy and his mission, but was quickly disappointed.

The people he had looked forward to seeing were busy with their own interests, and it was hard to find any group willing to listen to his plans and reasons for being there. He unburdened himself, as he so often had done, by writing to his cousin, Josiah Hale:

> New York City, September 27, 1852

> In respect to the special objects of my mission to the Atlantic States I cannot speak with much encouragement. I have not had the opportunity to present the cause publicly since I returned to the City.... Mr. [Henry Ward] Beecher has not yet found a place for it. Mr. Spear's people have not concluded to do anything.

> At times I feel like giving both institutions [Tualatin Academy and the Female Academy] up entirely...., I have toiled faithfully, and my wife, and Harvey Clark and his wife more so, for four years to establish these institutions.... We have now done all we can unless we have help to go on.

Atkinson knew teachers could be found, if only he could get the churches to pledge money for payment of bills. This had been the stumbling block in completing the Academy building in 1851, as the builder refused to do any more work until he was paid in full for the labor that had been done. Atkinson closed his letter by saying:

---

19   Atkinson, Nancy.

If my mission fails here it will be a death blow to my efforts for good to any considerable extent in Oregon. Not only was it difficult to get an audience with the ministers, but those interested enough to consider a gift tied such strings to their gifts that it created new difficulties and was almost useless.

Mr. R.W. Roper subscribed five hundred dollars to found a professorship of languages at our college provided $20,000 is raised for the purpose; that is, he is willing to give one twentieth of a Professorship. I have proposed to call it the Brooklyn Professorship.

The period of discouragement was rewarded shortly after the above letter was written. Dr. Badger and Dr. Theron Baldwin, the secretaries who had been instrumental in sending Atkinson to the Territory, came to his aid by promising to present his case to the Collegiate Society at its annual meeting in October. With relief, Atkinson was able to report:

Five months of waiting for that event was spent in soliciting aid for both institutions, and presenting their Home Missionary aspects and needs in sermons in New England, New York and Brooklyn churches. The result was a collection of over $4,000 in cash and books for school and library in both.

The American College and Education Society endorsed our college and put it ninth in its order in their list, and pledged the interest, six percent, of ten thousand dollars for the salary of our first college professor.

This pledge of money by the American College and Education Society was continued until 1860. And, it made a world of difference to the future of Tualatin Academy.

At last, the ministers rallied and prepared a circular for distribution. It was signed by the Trustees of the Academy; by Dr. Badger and D.B. Coe, secretaries of the American Home Missionary Society; the prominent clergymen R.S. Storrs, Jr., Henry Ward Beecher, Gardiner Spring, George B. Cheever, William Adams, Thomas Skinner, Samuel H. Cox and Edwin F. Hatfield; and by the prominent book publishers, Mark H. Newman, Henry Ivison and A.S. Barnes and Co.

Atkinson had come East with two responsibilities. He had finally succeeded in one by getting the financial backing of the churches and ministers. Now, he turned to his second endeavor.

He had been commissioned to return with a professor capable of teaching in the college, and with the potential later of becoming head of the institution at Forest Grove.

Success seemed assured, for a young man was found who appeared interested and who spent the next several weeks studying textbooks and thinking through the responsibilities he would face in the Oregon country. Then, he abruptly changed his mind! However, he did introduce Atkinson to another, Sidney Harper Marsh, a student from Union Theological Seminary, who he said might be interested.

Marsh had gone from Union Theological Seminary to Leesburg Academy because the southern climate was healthier for him than the cold of the northern states. He was finishing his second year as Assistant Principal and teacher in Leesburg Academy, Leesburg, Virginia, when he met Atkinson. He was decidedly cordial to the idea, and Atkinson found the candidate to his liking, saying, "He has the staying qualities of stick-to-it-iveness."

Sidney Marsh resigned his post at Leesburg, and the Board of Trustees voted

> To express to Mr. Marsh our regret at the severance of the connextion [sic] which has existed between us – our respect and regard for him personally, and our entire approbation of the manner in which he has conducted the Academy.

> W. H. Gray, President
> Thomas P. Knox, Secretary[20]

Marsh then contacted individuals to whom he might report on his new venture at a later date. One detailed request was sent to Spencer F. Baird, Esq., at the "Smithsonian Institute" in Washington, D.C.

> New York Dec 15th, 1852

> Dear Sir:

> As it will be impossible for me to visit Washington before my departure for Oregon I take the liberty to make use of the accompanying letter to introduce the object for which I now write you.

---

20   Sidney Harper Marsh Collection, Pacific University.

I go to Oregon to make a commencement of the first institution of the higher kind in the Territory. Its beginnings are small enough but the demand for it is such and with the condition and prospects of the country in which it is situated that there can be little doubt of its success.

Tualatin College [*sic*] is chartered, has a commodious and sufficiently large building with 160 acres of land and is hereafter to be under the care and receive the assistance of the "Collegiate Society." It is finely situated both with reference to healthfulness and natural scenery at "Forrest Grove" [*sic*] in the Willamette Valley about 25 miles distant from Oregon City. I wish to take out with me some of the most needful books as a nucleus for a library of the institution, and am now trying with good success so far to get the means to purchase such together with some little apparatus. It would greatly assist me in accomplishing my object if you could give it a bit of your Smithsonian Publications and also the instruments for meteorological and other observations.

Exactly what would be the value of such observations there I do not know but believe that there have been none taken in exactly that region where I am going except with such instruments as the missionaries happened to have. Any hints as to points of particular interest I should be thankful for, and so far as I can be glad to increase the knowledge of that imperfectly known country.

Very respectfully yours
S.H. Marsh

P.S. It is desirable that anything I am to take with me should reach here before the 24th inst. They may be directed so as to remain in the express office until called, and a letter directed to the care of Abner Benedict, Esq., 64 John St., N.Y. will be forwarded to me.

S.H. Marsh[21]

---

21   *Ibid.*

Sidney Harper Marsh, it appeared, was a man who would shape the destiny of the institution in Oregon, a rare person who formed history rather than reacting to it.

Chapter 9
Birth of the College: 1853-1858

George Atkinson returned to Oregon and his family, feeling that his accomplishments in the East had been fruitful. He was eager to report to the Trustees about the new president who would be joining them in 1853.

Not only had Atkinson found a man who had been successful in an academy in the East, but one who was young—28 years of age—and enthusiastic in founding a college.

Sidney Harper Marsh was the third generation in an illustrious family that had changed the face of higher education in America. He had graduated from the University of Vermont, where his father was president. Growing up in a college president's home gave him ideas of how a college program should work. Too, he had grown up on the story of his grandfather, Eleazer Wheelock, who a generation before had founded an Indian school in Connecticut. Eleazer Wheelock had then petitioned Lord Dartmouth in England for land on which to found a "school of higher learning." Lord Dartmouth gave him the land in present-day Hanover, New Hampshire. The Indian school was moved there, and Wheelock helped clear the land on which to build his school, Dartmouth College. With this example, according to Atkinson, Sidney Marsh should be equal to any experience he might face.

However, Sidney Marsh was not physically pre-possessing, being average in height, dark haired, and wearing steel-rimmed glasses to correct weak eyesight. Whatever his physical limitations might appear to have been, he was studious and determined in character.

Finally, Sidney Marsh was ready, with the accumulation of books and paraphernalia he had collected, and he set off for the West via the route across the Isthmus of Panama.

On June 14, 1853, the Portland newspaper announcement read: "Arrived early Tuesday morning from San Francisco, Steam propeller Fremont", and among the passengers listed was one "Mr. S. Marsh."

Tualatin Academy and Forest Grove were twenty miles west, and could only be reached by corduroy roads that were heavy with dust in the summer and, as Marsh would learn later, deep in mud in the winter or the rainy season. The corduroy roads were made of logs laid crosswise from side to side, and then covered with dirt to keep them firmly in place. The roads also were obviously bumpy to riders in wagons.

Either Atkinson or Clark met Marsh and took him and his belongings to Forest Grove. Sidney Marsh was pleased with the location on arrival, and reported:

> The Tualaty Plain was highly favored by nature, and had been sparsely
> occupied, a square mile apiece for the settlers. It was a beautiful location,
> near Gales Creek, Gales peak in the background; rolling ground covered
> with scattered oaks and thick firs that were mostly to disappear.[1]

Sidney Harper Marsh's attention then turned to the single frame Academy building. A second classroom had just been finished on the first floor; the second floor remained unfinished.

The log church was still being used for classes, and it is supposed that the log home for students under Tabitha Brown's guidance was still an active part of the campus.

Marsh took his meals at Alvin Smith's home, a good mile and a half south of the campus, across the swale by way of the foot bridge.

Since there was no home for the new president, he took over the unfinished second floor of the Academy building. One section became Marsh's study and living quarters, with his bed on the unfinished beams; the other section became the library for his books. The first book placed on the shelf was *The History of Harvard University*, given by a benefactor of the growing institution, Rev. Damon of the Sandwich Islands.

Mr. J.M. Keeler was Principal of the Academy when Marsh arrived. It was made up of students of all ages. Marsh represented the college, and in effect *was* the college, since there were no college-age students when he arrived. In this situation, he set about to create a student body, realizing

---

1   Sidney Harper Marsh Collection.

that he might have to wait for the Academy students to grow to college age unless some of college age moved into the area.

On April 12 and 13, Alvin Smith reported that he "attended meeting of the Trustees of Tualatin Academy and Pacific University. We adopted most of the articles of the Tualatin Academy."

Marsh realized that his inauguration as President was essential before the chartering of the College should take place. He spent many hours on his address, feeling it must express his beliefs in the future of the new college. May 3, 1854, was the date of the inauguration. Marsh's son, James Wheelock Marsh, later reported that he thought the Inauguration took place at Alanson Hinman's store near the campus.[2] But Robertson, in his *Origin of Pacific* written in 1905, stated that it was held outdoors on the campus.[3]

Regardless of the place where the Inauguration was held, we can be sure it was a major event for people of the town and the surrounding area. It is safe to assume the Trustees were in attendance, along with faculty and students of the Academy, members of the church and other interested friends of this great undertaking.

The Inaugural address, which Marsh called a Discourse, was dignified and gives a thoughtful expression of the college he envisioned:

> Today, Pacific University commences its formal and public organization, accepts publicly and solemnly its responsibilities, and assumes a position from which there is no honorable retreat. After five years of preparation, of painful and strenuous effort, this institution takes a step in advance; the idea of education has taken a higher form of development; the Academy has become the College.

In developing this theme, he laid out his ideas which make up the basic plan for a college:

> The essential of true learning is *wisdom*. The University and Collegiate systems are avowedly for the accomplishment of this object, to find an evidence of the intrinsic worth of learning. They are to advance true learning – they acknowledge no other end.

---

2   James Wheelock Marsh: Reminiscences to the author.
3   Robertson, J.R.: *Origin of Pacific University*, 1905.

In this Institution we humbly hope that this idea of a true and manly culture may be realized. It is a purpose which calls for all our energy; a design large enough to employ all our philanthropy. Were it merely to teach the sciences and formal knowledge, its establishment would be of interest and importance. But when we consider that the design involves not only the discipline of talents but the evolution of character – that to make MEN, and not mere scholars is our purpose...that we here, almost within hearing of the roar of the Pacific in this land so recently a wilderness; that we, the first, not in haste but with deliberation, and to meet the exigencies of the country, not heedlessly, but prayerfully, are publicly organizing a College – we feel that neither energy, nor philanthropy, nor any human power can suffice to accomplish what is undertaken. We feel it a privilege as well as a duty to be able to commit this institution, consecrated in its infancy, now, in the first flush and vigor of manhood, to that God who *has* guarded and guided, and who will, we hope and pray, yet crown it with his praise.[4]

The incorporation in Oregon took place the next month, June 1854, with a new charter. While the Incorporation document now read: President and Trustees of Pacific University and Tualatin Academy, it duplicated the Academy charter, with the ability to hold land and capital stock increased to a "township of land and $500,000."

It is interesting to note this passage of Tualatin Academy to Pacific University and take a moment to describe the naming of the university. It was Marsh who chose the name Pacific University, rather than either of the two other names—Columbia or Washington—that had been suggested.

Mr. Marsh had come West to "found a college," but on his arrival in Forest Grove he envisioned a larger future for the school than a college. For the first time, Marsh had used "Pacific University" in his Inaugural Discourse, and the new charter that followed gave the institution the opportunity to become, when the time was right, a university with more than one college program. He was a man with a dream beyond physical ability at this time.

October 1853 brought a new problem, as Alvin Smith, Rev. John Griffin and Rev. William Geiger asked the Forest Grove church to call a council about "getting a new minister." While Alvin Smith was the only one who was a local church member in Forest Grove, both Griffin and Geiger were

---

4   Marsh, S.H.: Inaugural discourse. A complete copy is in the Marsh
     Collection, Pacific University.

Congregationalists and members of other churches in the denomination. The latter two joined with Smith to bring the matter to a vote. It was not so much a matter of removing Clark as it was their desire to set down roots and have a church as they had known it before and to have a minister who only ministered. Though these were church matters, they affected Academy attendance, for Smith had enrolled the children who lived with him in a school on the East Plain in the fall of 1853 and 1854, as he had done in 1851 to express his disapproval.

George Atkinson, aware of the church problems about to erupt, moved quickly to solve the problem. He conferred first with Clark, and then talked with Naylor, the church clerk. Following these visits, Mr. Atkinson wrote to the American Home Missionary Society in the East, enclosing a copy of the Resolution that Naylor provided from the Forest Grove church and their written request for a new minister. This new minister, according to the request signed by Naylor, would be promised a salary of $400 per year.

Atkinson continued his report to the Board:

> That [the Forest Grove church] is the oldest church of our order in Oregon. Rev. H. Clark, who has ministered to it for 10 years, feels unable to do so longer. He will leave them shortly, or as soon as a man comes, and travel about more as a missionary. In this work we need him very much and we are confident that he is the man to do it best, while also he will be acting for our Institution.[5]

George Atkinson had served his co-worker, Harvey Clark, and at the same time given the church a way out of an embarrassing situation. He had also made use of the talent Clark had for working with and loving people. As Atkinson went about organizing new Congregational churches in Oregon and Washington, Clark helped build and nurture them—with a salary now of $600 a year.

Clark's resignation was accepted, and on April 1, 1854, Rev. Thomas Condon, who was recommended by the American Home Missionary Society in the East, became the pastor.

Thomas Condon, the new minister, was a talented man thirty-two years of age. He had been born in Ireland in 1822, immigrated with his family to America in 1833 and arrived in Oregon in 1852. He was available to become the minister to the Forest Grove church when he was called in 1854.

---

5   Atkinson, George H., Chicago Theological Seminary.

There is no information, however, about his having served earlier in other churches, so this may have been his only ministry. The church served his needs in other ways, for his interests proved to lie mainly in the field of geology.

There had been geological findings in the John Day area of Eastern Oregon. Some gold had been discovered by miners, as well as fossils that the miners had turned over to men like Condon for study.

Here in the hills was where Condon's true interests lay. Happily, he also found that he could call on Marsh or Clark to preach for him while he went out to dig for fossils. He reported to the American Home Missionary Society that "Mr. Clark and Prof. Marsh, now President of our University, both preach occasionally."[6] In another report to the Home Missions office, he stated, "As far as my engagements here are concerned this (traveling to different sites) will become easy owing to Mr. Clark's improved health."

In September 1855, a year later, Condon resigned from his church, saying that Rev. Elkanah Walker had started another church in Forest Grove, "twenty yards distant from the Clark's [church]. Also the people considered a preacher who did not farm effeminate and lazy."[7]

Apparently, the local church did not give full appreciation to Thomas Condon's preferred vocation of geology. Within ten years of having left the ministry, Condon had discovered the fossil remains of a prehistoric three-toed horse and many other fossils of great paleontological importance. He was to return later to Pacific University as Professor of Natural Sciences and as a well-known authority on geologic formations.[8]

It is true that Condon's final problem in 1855 was due to Elkanah Walker's having founded a Constitutional Presbyterian Church of West Tualatin Plain at his home. However, it had just three members—Walker, his wife, Mary, and Henry C. Raymond. With Condon's departure, the Walker church was not heard of again.

Meanwhile, President Marsh proceeded to plan for a faculty. His first choice was appointing Rev. Horace Lyman to the chair of Mathematics; later, he would be transferred to History and Rhetoric. Rev. Lyman and Marsh had long known each other, and Rev. Lyman had founded the Portland Congregational Church. Now he was willing to join President Marsh

---

6   Condon, Thomas, Chicago Theological Seminary.

7   *Ibid.*

8   Robertson, J.R., *Origin of Pacific University.*

in building the University. He was a good and understanding teacher and, because he believed in the principles Marsh wanted to instill in the school, he was a most satisfactory Acting President when Marsh was to make trips East for financial support.[9]

The population arriving from the East was increasing, but the lots in Forest Grove sold slowly. Since they were the "endowment" for the growth of the Tualatin Academy and Pacific University, more money had to be raised from interested individuals. Both Marsh and Atkinson increased their correspondence with friends, relatives and church leaders that they had met in Eastern church circles. In 1854, a year after Marsh had come west, it had even been suggested by another community that perhaps Pacific should be moved there where the town was larger and more conducive to education. The Forest Grove community reacted quickly. The trustees declined the invitation to move, and the town members gave of their resources to help the Academy hold its own financially during this challenging period.

One other change in leadership in the Academy is worth noting at this time. In 1855, Mr. Keeler and his wife, who was "preceptress" of the young ladies, went to California for her health. To succeed Keeler as Principal of the Academy, Marsh sought out Erasmus D. Shattuck, a fellow Vermonter 31 years of age. It was a good choice for the Academy, because, like Marsh, Shattuck believed in education, was studying law and was strong-minded. They made a good team and Shattuck, in later years, went on to become one of the most respected jurists in Oregon.

Distinct changes had taken place in the ten years since the Clarks and Smiths had settled in the West. Where the early years had seen the emerging Oregon Territory and state dependent on the ministers and few settlers working together as needs arose, government had now come into its own, moving from a headquarters in Oregon City to Salem, a more centrally located part of the developing state.

Earlier, too, where there was misunderstanding between the Tualatine tribe of Kalapooians and the settlers, the sub-Indian agent had turned to clergymen like Harvey Clark for help. Now, the sub-Indian agent dealt directly with the Indian leaders and the governing body in Salem. It was a bitter time for the Indians, whose chiefs sought to keep their homes and resisted efforts to move them east. They were not fighters, but finally asked only for the area around Wapato Lake, an area that was home to them and that provided their foods in good supply. But the pressure of increasing pop-

---

9   *Ibid.*

ulation was too much, and the Indians were forced to the eastern part of Oregon—strange territory to them.[10]

This matter of Indians (apart from the Tualatines) being displaced by white settlers came to a head in the fall of 1855. The state of affairs had a strong impact on education, government and church affairs when the Yakima Indians struck unexpectedly at settled areas east of the Cascades.

The settlers, their representatives and the military hoped to contain the fighting beyond the Cascades so the Willamette Valley would not be endangered. However, if the Indians came West the more settled areas in Washington and Oregon would be subject to the conflict.

The older Indians in the Wapato Lake area south of Forest Grove did not want war with their neighbors, but the young men of the tribe saw this as a chance to get rid of the settlers who had taken their land. The elders counseled their youth not to be hasty.

Those white men who were able-bodied went East to fight, using the less strong men to make a second line of defense at the Cascades. This left the women, children, the old and the infirm to protect their homes.[11]

On the West Tualatin Plain, men began to dig trenches around the Academy building and the Catching home one mile east of the campus. The belfry on the Academy became the tower lookout for approaching enemies, using the tower bell to warn the settlers if there was danger. Then they began construction of a fort.

Mrs. Elkanah Walker in her diary made this notation:

Sunday, Oct. 21 (1855) Ministers and deacons all at work on the fort, no meeting

Oct. 23 Folks still at work on the fort. Mrs. Brown is peeved because the fort was not built around the Academy.

There was, of course, good reason why the fort was not built around the Academy building. There were too many large, old oak trees, and for tactical reasons the fort had to stand on high ground with a clear view and command of open space.

---

10   *Ibid.*
11   Kalapooians, Carey.

Not far south of the Forest Grove campus where preparations were taking place, Capt. Absalom Hembree was gathering a company of volunteers to move east to the Yakima war at the Cascades. Capt. Hembree lived on a Donation Land Claim a few miles from the present town of Gaston. Originally hailing from Tennessee, he had come from Missouri in the migration of 1843. Joining quickly in the life of the territory, he was a member of the Oregon provisional legislature from 1846 through 1848, and then served as a member of the territorial legislature in 1849, and 1851 through 1854. He was not an Army man, but persuaded volunteers to join him and became "captain" of the group.

As the Captain and his men passed down the road, neighbors lined up at the fence and cheered as long as the company was in sight.

Some days later, the company had arrived in the area where the struggle had been taking place. Capt. Hembree went out with a group of his men to reconnoiter. They saw a peaceful scene in the meadow ahead, with stray horses scattered about grazing. Suddenly they became aware that behind each horse was an Indian, rising up and ready for the kill. Indian strategy was something these settlers and their leaders had not anticipated. Capt. Hembree was killed, but not before he had killed two Yakimas. The volunteers, well-trained, fought hard and repulsed the small band. One of them killed the Indian who had already taken Capt. Hembree's scalp, and retrieved it to be put with the Captain's body.

We are fortunate to have the story as witnessed by a six-year-old boy, Alfred Kenny, who lived in the Wapato Lake area near the Hembree land claim. He later recounted the story in a letter to his niece, Mary Drain Albro. After telling about the Hembree company passing by his orchard on their way to battle, he wrote:

> As the following weeks passed one morning a "squaw man" who lived with
> the indians at Wapato Village came to our house and said the indian chief
> told him Capt. Hembrees Company was fought by the indians and Capt. was
> killed.[12]

---

12   Kenny, Alfred: Letter sent to Mary Drain Albro, a niece, who gave a copy to
      the author. These were the experiences of a young boy who later became a
      physician. Mrs. Albro, a friend of Pacific, had a pioneer rose garden planted
      on the campus near Warner Hall during Dr. Giersbach's presidency.

It's worth noting that a "squaw man" was a white or non-Indian who lived with or married an Indian woman and lived in her village.

This news made the younger Twalatine Indians more restless, and the older ones did their best to control the "young bucks," as Alfred called them, lest there be bloodshed on their home territory. Alfred Kenny's letter continues:

> Then one night near bedtime, a [k]nock at our door, mother opened it and in walk an old squaw who sometimes worked for Mother, followed with three old indians with guns. The squaw said the young bucks wanted to take every white scalp and they had come to defend us.
>
> Mother told them to lay down with their feet on the hearth on our big fireplace. She then reached up and took down the shot gun, drew up her chair to the corner of the hearth, renewed the fire with some more oak wood, and sat there all night with the gun across her knees, knitting. I was laying on the floor at her feet, Marshall on the other. I would look up at her face. She seemed unconcerned, was not speaking a word; give no sign of fear. Albert, then 12 years had taken a rifle, and planted himself outside the house behind an oak tree where he could watch all approach. Jane sat on the bottom step of the stairs. Gus took a seat by a window to watch the road, the two younger children were in bed – so in quiet we passed the night, not a word spoken all night, the squaw and the indians on the floor asleep. In the morning when the chickens began to crow, Mother in a low voice began to sing "How Firm a Foundation." Then with the coming of day our indian defenders got up and filed out and away.

One wonders how many other homes were defended as this one was. Again, one can appreciate the stoic women who lived through such experiences in those early days.

Word came to the neighborhood that Capt. Hembree was being brought home for burial, and neighbors again stood by the fence at the orchard to pay their respects.

Alfred's story continues:

> The wagon with his body halted, the lid of the box raised off. Mother and my Aunt Maria stepped to the side of the wagon and seemed to be doing something. I noticed Mother reached into her hand bag and take out a threaded needle and I have always had the impression that she was stitching his scalp in place – for when Capt. Hembree fell an indian scalped him, but

soon after that indian was killed and Capts scalp recovered. When Mother stepped from the wagon then orderly all stepped up for a glimpse. The wagon moved on.

Several days later, Capt. Hembree's body was buried on his land claim with a marker. The Kenny family wanted a large monument for their hero, but at the time the Oregon legislators did nothing, suggesting that there were many fallen heroes and favoritism should be avoided. It should be noted, however, that a monument was erected in 1920 in the Cascades area where Hembree fell.

As the Yakima war waged on in eastern Washington Territory, a group of young men in the Puget Sound area were enlisted to go out and "subjugate the Indians" wherever they might be found. One of these young men was Harvey Scott, who later would become part of the life at Pacific University. His service of enlistment lasted from October 1855 to August 1856. Through that year, he never lost sight of the dream of obtaining more of the education that was postponed when his family had taken the trail West in 1852. A quick visit to the Forest Grove campus in 1853 made him aware that this was the place to which he must return.

Scott left Olympia on foot on September 30, 1856, with a little less than $80.00, saved from working in a lumber camp. It took a week for him to reach Portland. Walking on to Yamhill County, Scott got a job at "farm labor," and in two months had added almost $40.00 to take with him to Forest Grove.

On arrival at the campus, Scott asked where the head of the Academy could be found. He was told to look for Shattuck on his way to the Academy where he was expected. On the street, Harvey Scott stopped a man who he felt sure would be Shattuck, and asked if it were he. Shattuck said yes and explained that it was the middle of the term, but maybe Scott could fill the requirement for the whole term. And so Harvey Scott entered the Academy, and with it a friendship with Erasmus Shattuck that was to last many years.

Harvey Scott met three students there, Marion F. Mulkey, a J.W. Johnson and a fellow named Leach, who had just started on the College Course. Leach did not continue in the course, and Mulkey and Johnson soon decided to go east to Yale University, since at this time there were only two college faculty members, Prof. Lyman and President Marsh. This was a disappointment to Marsh, of course, but he prepared Mulkey and Johnson for their Yale requirements and sent them east with his blessing.[13]

(Both men returned to the West after graduating from Yale in 1862. Marion Mulkey became a much-respected lawyer in Portland. J.W. Johnson became assistant adjutant of Washington Territory in 1862. In 1869, he established the Portland High School. And in 1872, he served as secretary of the convention of Liberal Republicans at which Horace Greeley was nominated for President. Afterward, he became President of the University of Oregon.)

Ever mindful of the needs of a college program, Marsh was concerned about choosing something beyond the classes the students attended. A debating society might create new independent thinking, he reasoned. But in establishing this new intellectual pursuit he discovered there were not enough older students to make up two teams. As a result, Marsh invited townspeople to join his debating society. Each month, he prepared a title for debate and assigned parts to his two teams. One of the popular debaters was Milton Tuttle, important in secular and political affairs and Justice of the Peace. He always took part. Usually, Samuel Hughes, the town's blacksmith, served also as a popular member on the teams. These debates were always attended by students as well as the community. Eventually, the debating society became the Gamma Sigma Literary Society.[14]

With the beginning of 1856, the members of the Congregational Church were keenly aware that the log church, doubling during the week as the school, was definitely showing signs of age. An agreement was reached whereby the church could rent the Academy building for Sunday services for $50.00 a year. So, for one year it became their meeting house while plans were being made to build a church off-campus. As for ministers after Thomas Condon's resignation, Harvey Clark, Sidney Marsh and Elkanah Walker served from 1855 to 1856. From 1856 to 1861, Cushing Eells succeeded Harvey Clark.[15] The college and church continued to work as one, and the town was served by the Trustees of the University until it would grow large enough to have its own elected governing body.

In spite of President Marsh's trying to fill the young minds of his charges with noble thoughts, there were pranks that only the young could devise. One of these pranks had to do with the bell in the Academy belfry that rang to begin class periods and for the compulsory chapel services. One

---

13   *Ibid.*
14   Scott, Harvey W.
15   *Ibid.*

day, however, the bell did not ring, and upon studying the situation it was discovered that the clapper of the bell was missing. Shortly afterward, the firewood piled in a shed near the Academy also disappeared. The wood was found in the well near the building. Students were detailed to get the wood back where it belonged, and at the end of the task, the clapper of the bell was also found at the bottom.

The students thought it had been fun, but the adults were less than amused by the prank.[16]

Some students did have ideas, however, that probably pleased President Marsh. There were no printing presses available, so the group planning a student newspaper had to write each copy by hand, and the articles were read to the students by an editor. Several copies of these early editions—dated Dec. 11, 1857, Dec. 28, 1857, and Jan. 1858—were found in the safe in Marsh Hall in 1940.

The *Rosebud*, made up of student compositions, was published by the young ladies of the Academy. The *Star of the West* was edited by the young men. The *Star* appeared with a grand statement of purpose—and a lack of punctuation. The first issue was dated December 29, 1858, though they may possibly have meant 1857, since it was the first issue of volume one. Its editor, Marcus W. Walker (Elkanah's son), established the publication's objective:

Prospectus

The Star of the West is published at Forest Grove once in two weeks by the Students of Tualatin Academy and is devoted to Literature Art and Science

Editorial columes

In presenting you with the first no. of the Star of the West we do it with no feelings of pride or desire to display our talents & abilities no we are too modest for that but we wish to try to do something for the public good We have long noticed a defect in the literary world of Forest Grove and we consider it our duty to remedy it and judging from the communications we have received we will do it for they are just what is wanted of the very highest literary character & display a genius which we did not suppose existed in the community.

---

16   History of the Congregational Church, Forest Grove, OR.

Our columes will ever be open to Art Science & Literature & every thing which would be interesting to an intelligent community like ours We advocate no Policies of any kind of whatever name or character

We expect and shall realize a large patronage We have been told by persons who have run a few of poorest communications that they far surpass their highest expactations.

The articles that followed were illustrated Christian Honesty, Knowledge, Metals & their uses, etc.[17]

By 1857, the Alvin Smiths had built a white frame house near the place where the Carnation mill now stands. That same year, the Clarks were able to move north, closer to the campus, and enjoy a white frame house which had been built by Sidney H. Marsh on a lot he bought.[18] He was glad to sell it to Harvey Clark, and Mrs. Clark must have been happy to be in a comfortable home at last, with their four growing children—three daughters and a son, James Harvey. The younger son had not lived beyond infancy.

The Academy and College were making progress, though money was still the major worry. There was a faculty of three, with the third person, Shattuck, teaching in both the Academy and College.

The church leaders had been looking for a place off-campus on which to build a new church, but the sites did not seem just right. Then, Elkanah Walker had a suggestion. There were lots across from the campus owned by Cushing Eells, which would do nicely; if Cushing Eells would trade those lots for some of the Walker property, equally good, Walker would give the Eells lots to the church for a building. The lots were "south of President Marsh's house on the Prairie." The church accepted the offer. Walker gave his lots to Eells; however, the Eells lots were deeded directly to the church. This created the question over the years as to who really gave the lots to the church. The church minutes of July 1857, though, contain a resolution "accepting the offer of Elkanah Walker, for the lots formerly owned by Cushing Eells."[19]

---

17 James Wheelock Marsh: Reminiscences.
18 Student papers: Marcus Walker, editor, later worked for the *San Francisco Pacific*.
19 James Wheelock Marsh: Reminiscences.

The church lot ran all the way south to what is now Pacific Avenue. The church was a beautiful white New England-style building, with a steeple, facing south. The approach to the church, up the slight incline, was inspiring. In 1859, the new church was dedicated, and built at a cost of $7,000. One thousand dollars was pledged in the beginning by Alvin Smith if the church were built according to his plan.

If 1857 was a year of beginnings—the students' burgeoning academic efforts and a new church and homes—it was also a time of endings. Grandma Brown had gone to Salem, where her family members welcomed her. However, townspeople in Forest Grove were saddened that year by news of her death at 77 years of age.

Her long friend and co-worker, Harvey Clark, continued as President of the Board of Trustees, with George Atkinson serving as its Secretary. But Harvey Clark's lack of strength no longer enabled him to carry out the details that his mind tried to force on his body. For the last several springs, he had been ill with "pulmonary troubles" which finally took their toll. In 1858, he was less able to carry on the Home Missionary visits.

When a friend was lamenting Clark's illness and the fact that he had given away 350 acres of land, Harvey Clark answered, "I do not wish for much land. I wish the school to prosper."[20] On March 24, 1858, Harvey Clark, pioneer missionary, died at 9 p.m.

One of the Walker's sons, a student at the Academy, watched as the pallbearers brought Harvey Clark's casket out of the house. A white fence surrounded the house, with a stile that protected the property from wandering animals.

S.T. Walker remembered much of this man:

> I well remember his funeral which took place from the house now owned by Mrs. Littlehales. Instead of a gate there was a stile. I remember there was some difficulty in getting the coffin over it.

Harvey Clark was buried in the pioneer cemetery, on a hill overlooking Forest Grove and the University.

Two days later, his friend, Atkinson, who had shared ten years of labor with him in establishing Tualatin Academy and Pacific University, preached the funeral sermon. He followed it with a memorial service at the Academy that afternoon.

---

20   History of the Congregational Church.

The Board of Trustees, in their minutes April 14, had this to state:

> Mr. Clark died March 24, 1858, of consumption aged fifty-five years. From
> the first, nearly ten years, he has been President of the Board, and for about
> nine years its agent, responsible in great measure for the debts. The
> following resolutions were passed:

> Whereas it has pleased God to remove by death Rev. Harvey Clark the
> President of the Board of Trustees:

> Resolved – That while we humbly submit to this mysterious dispensation of
> Providence, we would express our sense of the great loss which this
> Institution has sustained in his death. We would also bear testimony to the
> many labors and sacrifices which Brother Clark cheerfully made through ten
> years to establish this Institution.

> Resolved – that we shall ever cherish his name in grateful remembrance.[21]

The *Oregon Argus* of Hillsboro printed an obituary that also supported this
rare individual's altruism:

> There [in Tualatin Plains] he not only performed the duties of a pastor and
> preacher for ten years, but he began to establish an institution of learning,
> first called an Orphan Asylum and now styled Tualatin Academy and Pacific
> University. To promote the object of this school he gave 200 acres of his
> claim and then disposed of 150 more with reference to the same object.[22]

Atkinson paid tribute to Harvey Clark in an article written for *The Home
Missionary* magazine published in September, titled " Good Man Gone."[23]
He provided additional insight into the power that drove this man, stating,
"indeed, he was never physically strong. The native power of his mind kept
him up, and bore him through many labors and trials under which ordinary
minds, in such a body, would have sunk." "He wore out early," Atkinson
said. "A neighbor, not a religious man, who had known him for eleven

---

21   Hillsboro, OR, *Argus*.
22   Trustee Records.
23   *Home Missionary* magazine, September 1858.

years, said, 'I have loved Mr. Clark more than I have loved any man in Oregon. He was always the same. He lived to benefit the whole community.' This is his record among people."

Another tribute, by William H. Gray in his *History of Oregon*, published in 1870, reflects the feelings of one man who had known Clark since he had arrived at the Whitman Mission in 1840, and had worked with him through the days of Champoeg when a form of government was a must:

> Rev. Harvey Clark was a man whose religion was practical, whose labors were without ceasing, of slender frame, black hair, deep mellow voice, kind and obliging to all.
>
> Mr. Clark is perhaps the best man that could have been sent with the early settlers. He early gained their confidence and esteem, and was always a welcome visitor among them. He had not that stern commanding manner which is usual to egotists of the clerical order, but was of the mild, persuasive kind that wins the rough heart and calms the stormy passions.
>
> The country is blessed by his having lived in it.[24]

---

24 Gray, William H.

Chapter 10
Growth of the College: 1859-1866

It had been nearly five years since Sidney Marsh had come to Oregon, and while it took time to get college-age students for his program, he had not lost heart. In fact, it would be another year until the next student entered Pacific. He had been sorry to lose Mulkey and Johnson, but could take pride in the fact that he had prepared them and Yale had accepted them as students. Shortly, Harvey Scott would be ready for college admission in 1859.

President Marsh knew he must go east and it would be at least a year before he could return. Money could only be procured if he was in the field to raise it. In late 1858, he conferred with Horace Lyman and laid his plans. Lyman would become acting president in his absence, and handle the courses for Harvey Scott in the coming year.

Marsh also wanted to have a home built for himself, and toward that end had purchased land across from the campus. He drew up the plans for the frame house, contracted Stephen Blank as builder and asked Lyman to keep an eye on progress.

As he had come west in 1853, now Marsh in 1858 reversed his steps, down the West Coast, across the Isthmus of Panama and up the East Coast to New York. The long trip gave him time to make listings—of individuals and churches he must visit in hopes of securing money as well as the College Education Society and its secretary, Rev. Theron Baldwin. He also made lists of books, scientific equipment and material, and library acquisitions. Of course, the search for money and large pledges was uppermost in priority. The money would be used for salaries for the college faculty and was the driving force behind his trip. His strategy was to concentrate his search in Boston and New York, areas where he was well known.

In Boston, Marsh wrote to Bro. Eells on October 20, 1859, telling him he had seen the Eells family members as requested. He followed with a report on his fundraising and the leaders in the denomination and local churches:

> I think I shall succeed.... If the good opinion of Dr. N. Adams, Dr. Kirk, Dexter Haskell and others could secure the $10,000 I ask here I should get it very soon, but money is very hard to get for any cause [his underscores] & for such as this very hard [double underscores].

> There will still be need of great economy of labor at the Grove - I will take a month possibly here & a month in N.Y. & then I hope to return. I am always home sick. If my horse is alive & any one wants him it will be as well to have him sold & any body may sell him who will be responsible to me for what they receive.[1]

On Oct. 25, he wrote at great length to Josiah Hale, cousin of George Atkinson, about his meeting in the Old South Church Chapel, an invitational affair with Congregational leaders and ministers at which his goal was suddenly doubled.

> The result was highly gratifying to me. They expressed themselves satisfied of the importance of the work. They advised an effort to raise $20,000 & Mr. John Field & Mr. Abner Kingman pledged $1000 each toward that sum. I have great hopes of $1000 from Mr. John Tappan.[2]

Marsh went on to state that he had never heartily adopted a "three-year plan. It would be difficult to get professors whose salaries would last only three years, so my subscription reads thus: 'upon condition that the sum of $20,000 is secured in valid subscriptions payable on or before the first of March 1860.'"

Ten days later, Marsh reported to Hon. N. Borditch, a benevolent friend who was ill and could not attend the South Chapel meeting, asking for his

---

1   Pacific University, Sidney Harper Marsh Collection.
2   *Ibid.* Some of the ministers advised Marsh to ask for three-year subscriptions, payable within that period. This was not accepted by him, who said no one would be willing to teach at a college if the salary were limited to three years.

subscription and reporting, "We now have subscriptions during the summer about $7000 of the $20,000."[3]

As the subscription pledges came in, Marsh's mind turned to investments. Not only did a president have to raise the money, but he must be astute in its investment as well. He wrote to George Atkinson in Bro. Atkinson's capacity as Secretary of the Board of Trustees:

Boston, Nov. 10, 1859

Dear Sir:

I have heard nothing from Oregon for months & don't know but the country's submerged by lava from Mt. Hood – of which there was a reported irruption [sic]. I hope there will be soil enough left for Pacific University to stand upon – otherwise all my labors will be fruitless – whatever else may happen....

In view of the possibility of my success it is time to consider the mode of investment (though of the $20,000 it is quite likely that much will be paid by note drawing interest). Within two months or three I shall probably remit to Mr. Lyman a good deal that should be at once invested securely. It is the distinct understanding with subscribers that these finances are for the support of teachers & are not to go to pay debts or anything else.

A good deal of harm would result if they are in any way carelessly managed. It seems to me that four or five thousand might be safely invested at 10 per ct secured by mortgage on property of at least twice the value of the loan & I should suppose Corbett or Shattuck would be safe advisers. Our future prosperity depends upon the income from these funds.

I hope to hear from you as soon as possible in regard to Mr. Tappan's proposition. If the Board authorizes it I will examine the matter and use the best of my judgment with such advice as I can command without incurring expense.[4]

---

3   *Ibid.*
4   Pacific University Library.

At this time, no details had surfaced as to the Tappan proposition. Marsh had hoped for a pledge of $1,000 from Tappan.

Sometimes an unexpected interlude changes the course of a person's life, and this was the case when Rev. Nelson Haskell invited Marsh to come to his home in East Boston while he was in that area raising funds. It was there that he met Haskell's niece, Elizabeth Haskell. She was living at the Haskell home while attending school. Elizabeth was 18 years old, attractive and musically talented. It was perhaps natural that this lonely, still-young man should fall in love with her, and that she, fortunately, reciprocated. While Marsh continued to raise his pledges, she finished her year at school. In mid-May, they were married. Her parents in East Bloomfield, Ohio, happily accepted Marsh into the family.

Nelson Haskell expressed his best wishes in a letter to Marsh that also conveyed the possibility of increased pledges:

> 1860 1st Sat. in August – East Boston
>
> I rec'd a few days since an excellent letter from your young wife - I hope God will abundantly bless her to you.
>
> Our annual collection for colleges this year shall be yours when it is taken & I shall be glad to "share" once or twice more if I am able.[5]

In the spring of 1861, the $20,000 goal was met. Now it was time to return to Oregon. The Marshes would go across the Isthmus of Panama, while their furniture—including Elizabeth's beloved piano—would have to go by sea via the much longer route around Cape Horn.

As Sidney and Elizabeth left New York harbor, they heard news that Fort Sumter had been fired upon by Southern forces on April 12. Indeed, as they sailed south past the fort on April 22 they heard the shelling in the distance. This made the thought of war too close for comfort.

As the Marshes' ship made its way up the West Coast, Elizabeth—now Lizzie to her husband—became more eager to see the college, the new home Sidney had planned, everything, including the flowers that grew on campus, for flowers were one of her chief interests.

---

5   *Ibid.*

On arrival in Forest Grove, things were not as had been pictured in Sidney's description. Stephen Blank had built the Marsh house, but he had put the President's house on the campus instead of on the Marsh lot.

As fast as it was possible to move the new house across the road—now College Way—to the Marsh lot, it was done. Settling the home was left to Mrs. Marsh when furniture arrived, while President Marsh took up his teaching schedule with Harvey Scott. Prof. Lyman had carried on with the basics of mathematics and ancient history, while helping Scott in advanced Latin. Scott wrote that when Marsh returned

> He [Marsh] took up various parts of the work. In the Greek language and literature, in history and philosophy, in political economy and physics, my studies were guided by him.[6]

President Marsh and Prof. Lyman carried the college instruction, but Scott gained much in addition upon meeting Edward Tanner, who came west as Academy Principal in 1861. Tanner was 24 years old, a graduate of Illinois College, and he and Scott became fast friends. Many hikes were taken up Gales Peak, during which the pair carried pocket volumes of the classics to read and discuss. This opened a world of literary and historical materials which Scott absorbed.

On May 16, 1862, the first child was born to the Marshes, James Wheelock Marsh. That same year, the University of Vermont conferred an honorary doctorate of divinity on Sidney Harper Marsh.

Marsh had been pleased to see that the debating society he had started was still flourishing and felt it was time to give it recognition. He called it "Gamma Sigma"—for *Gnothen Secuton*, "Know Thyself"—and it became a permanent part of Pacific University. The slogan, "Once a Gamma, always a Gamma" has held true since its beginning.

Other societies followed—the Philomatheans for women, and Alpha Zeta for men.

While President Marsh had been in the East, many changes had taken place in Oregon. Politically, the Republican Party had been born back east, and it was working its way west with the coming of new settlers. This called for Oregonians to choose party affiliations, where previously all worked for the Oregon country on a nonpartisan basis.

---

6   Scott, Harvey W.

But a more pressing matter on the Tualatin Plain was the Civil War. It was no longer a remote event. After Sumter was shelled, President Lincoln issued a proclamation and asked the states for men to fill the Union quota for soldiers. The Oregonians were hesitant. They admitted there was a movement in the state to turn their backs on the Union and side with the Confederacy.[7]

It was announced in the Tualatin area that there would be a horse race—one horse named Union and the other Confederacy. This must have seemed a decisive event, for according to one story Marsh hurried toward the race. A woman stopped him, saying, "Why, Dr. Marsh, are *you* going to the horse race?" His answer as he vaulted a fence was, "Madam, this is no horse race. It's a riot!"

There seem to be no details as the outcome of the race, except that the political question was not resolved on the finish line of the racetrack.

A very disturbing development was the growth of a secret organization known as the Knights of the Golden Circle. This group of Confederacy sympathizers was growing stronger with the passing of time as it strove to have Oregon join the Confederacy and create a Pacific Republic. By 1864, it had at least ten "circles," two of which were in Portland, with about 2,500 members.[8]

The older residents in the plain, leaning toward the Union, said they must have a home guard for protection from the Confederate sympathizers, and this was made up of students at Pacific University and settlers on Tualatin Plain. On December 1, 1864, a mass meeting of Washington County citizens was held at Tualatin Academy to recruit volunteers in support of the Union effort. As a result, "six companies were mustered in as the First Oregon Volunteer Infantry on June 23, 1865. All for naught: Lee surrendered more than two months before the formal muster as a regiment of Oregon infantry."[9]

In spite of the war atmosphere, Harvey Scott finished his college work, and in 1863 became Pacific's first graduate. There was no fancy program, but the graduation had dignity. Townspeople were invited to attend, Scott

---

7   Carey, Charles H., vol II. The material in the two volumes gives further details of both the Union and Confederate sides during the Civil War period.

8   *Ibid.*

9   *Ibid.* George Durham, a Pacific student, participated in the volunteer infantry. He later married a daughter of Harvey and Emeline Clark.

gave an oration and the A.B. degree was duly conferred upon him. Following the graduation ceremony, Dr. Marsh's next step was to create the Pacific University Alumni Association.

An Alumni Association was an important part of the College plan, essential for those about to graduate, but also to welcome graduates from other colleges who would later live in Oregon.

President Marsh knew that a third faculty member was needed, as the Academy was now producing future students for Pacific University. This influx of students called for more teachers, more equipment and more money. In 1863, Tanner was transferred from Academy to College status. A year later, he went back to Illinois College to teach, and B.G. Harpending joined the faculty. Harpending had been teaching for the past year at the Academy. His new duties were to succeed Tanner teaching science, ancient languages and literature. Professor Lyman was still teaching mathematics, and President Marsh became Professor of Intellectual, Political, and Moral Philosophy. With his classroom duties now lightened, President Marsh had time to develop the program he envisioned for the college.

Mrs. Marsh's talents also served to enrich the college life with her music. While Mr. Marsh was not musical, he knew the value of music and was overjoyed that his wife had become active. She was willing to teach piano when asked, and directed the church choir and developed group singing and cantatas. Seeing a need for additional voices, Mrs. Marsh enlisted the townspeople as well as campus students. In many ways, her efforts were the base on which Pacific's School of Music was built in 1885.[10]

In 1864, Mrs. Marsh gave birth to a daughter, Mary. While Miss Hodgden had come west with the Marshes to teach at the Academy, she proved helpful to Mrs. Marsh in the short emergency, and a student lived with the Marshes earning her room and board while at school.

The upper floor of the first building on campus was now finished, and the building was being filled to capacity. Another small unit, located on the southwest corner of the campus, was also called into service. It had been a storage building which was turned into the "den" for students while Harvey Scott had been a student; now it became a classroom.

Harvey Scott described the den "as he knew it" in 1861 when he returned to campus to speak in 1901.

---

10   James Wheelock Marsh: Reminiscences for the author.

At the southwest corner of the campus we had a little den which was used as a study and recitation room. The streets here then existed merely on paper; we made few rectangular movements, but cut sharply across lots....We had a path that ran upon a diagonal from the old building over to the little den. During two winters our school inhabited that little den most of the time. It was easy to keep warm, and we were fond of it. Professor Lyman came in and presided. There were a dozen, perhaps fifteen of us, of all grades of study.[11]

In 1865, it became apparent that the faculty needed to be increased again, since there would be three college graduates the following year and the same number to be graduated in 1867.

President Marsh employed Professor George H. Collier, an Oberlin graduate and a successful teacher and lecturer in the East, to teach chemistry, botany and geology. Marsh knew he would be away raising money, and offered the use of his home to the Colliers until their furniture arrived and they located a residence. The Colliers were expected in 1866 for the fall term.

Sidney Marsh was also overjoyed that his half-brother, Joseph Marsh, had finally agreed to join Pacific's faculty. Joseph had graduated from the University of Vermont and had subsequently taught in the East and in Canada. He would be a real asset to the Marsh program when he arrived in 1867.

President Marsh had also asked the Trustees to consider refurbishing the first building on campus—now Old College Hall—and building another for the growing institution. This was the beginning of a "sister" building to Old College Hall. Harvey Scott, working in Shattuck's law office, reported in the Portland *Oregonian* in 1866 that "a large new building was erected last year [1865], which with those formerly built, affords ample room for all purposes." He added, "Decidedly the largest and best library in Oregon belongs to Pacific University."[12] A few years later, Scott bought the *Ore-*

---

11   Scott, Harvey W.: Founders Day address, 1901. The address was also reported in the Portland *Oregonian*.

12   *Ibid.* After graduation in 1863, Scott studied law at Shattuck's offices in Portland. The *Oregonian*'s publisher at that time regularly stopped by to ask Shattuck to write something for his paper. One day, Shattuck suggested that

gonian, giving up the idea of law as a career and turning to writing and publishing.

The new building was very much in appearance like Old College Hall—now on the register of National Historic Buildings as the oldest college building used continually for instruction. It was a two-story frame building and had six finished rooms.

In February 1867, a student named Joseph Fish described the interior in a letter to Mrs. Marsh: "You wished to know how the rooms are finished in the new building. They are sealed with rough boards and white washed except from the floor upward about four feet. Six rooms are finished and four occupied."

Notes by Margaret Hinman, alumna and granddaughter of Trustee Chairman Alanson Hinman, give interesting details. "In 1865, a new Academy was built north of the original building and similar to it in structure. This burned in 1910. Chapel was upstairs in the Academy building with separate staircases for the boys and the girls. The History Room was back of the Chapel, while downstairs the Principal of the Academy had one large room and the Preceptress the other, and there again the boys came in from the East, the girls from the West."[13]

Scott write, and the ensuing article was well-received, leading to his regular contributions to the *Oregonian.*

13   Hinman, Margaret: Papers written for the author.

Chapter 11
Accomplishment: 1867-1870

With the faculty and college facilities under control by 1865, President Marsh was ready to make his second fund-raising trip east. This time he took his wife and two children with him. His family would be visiting Elizabeth's family, the Haskells, in Ohio while he labored in the Boston and New York areas.

The goal of $50,000 was stated in letters from Forest Grove to Marsh, a figure which his associates hoped he would raise although its achievement was never reported by President Marsh. A sizeable amount of money now, this target must have seemed almost unreachable then, but probably reflected the financial needs of the school very accurately.

On January 11, 1866, a student named J.E. Walker, son of Elkanah Walker, wrote a letter to Mrs. Marsh assuring her he was carrying on the church music in her absence. Then he wrote that the church needed a new minister, though his father said he would still preach until one was sent from the East.[1] Senator Corbett, a former Pacific Trustee now in Washington, wrote President Marsh at the same time, asking him to look around for a minister for the Grove while Marsh was in the East raising money.[2] Again, the close and continuing ties between school and church were made evident. The two institutions were still interdependent as in their beginnings.

More news came in George Atkinson's letter to President Marsh of August 31, 1866, reporting on the need for ministers in the West, scarce money and new Trustees for the University.

---

1   Sidney Harper Marsh Collection.

2   *Ibid.*

A College Grows in Oregon

Dear Bro.

During vacation matters at the Grove I am told were very quiet. The School has opened well with 25 in the College department.

I hear that you have got your first thousand dollar subscription. This is favorable. Whatever you get I would put into bonds at once, as the most convenient way of keeping it.

Of church matters you understand the condition. It is the same all around as when you left as far as I know. I hope you will meet men disposed to come out as the first Missionaries did to labor where providence shall direct. We expect Prof. C [Collier] as we saw a notice in the paper of a telegram about his coming.[3]

On October 15, 1866, a letter from Forest Grove to President Marsh congratulated him on the birth of a son, named Haskell, in Ohio, saying, "I shall insist on claiming him as an Oregonian."[4]

Finally, a letter came to Mrs. Marsh from Mrs. Collier, who had arrived with her husband. It is of interest because she seems so anxious to explain her husband and his adaptation to the new environment. This was perhaps a foreshadowing of events to come.

A new minister [Daniel Miles] arrived last week, we find him an excellent man.... A new library has been purchased for the Sabbath School & committee to procure new singing books.

Husband is to give an illustrated Philosophical Lecture before the Gamma Sigma next week. He is doing the best he can for the Institution and has not missed a recitation yet. He sometimes speaks of the wide reputation which he enjoyed in the states as an accurate thinker and accomplished teacher while here he is unknown, but I tell him that real effort will be appreciated if it is put forth in the name of the Master. We will do the best we can by your house and furniture. As far as we get things of our own we put yours carefully away. We find your home very comfortable and pleasant.

---

3   *Ibid.*
4   *Ibid.*

I suppose since you are released from teaching and other public labors which you performed here you find more time for reading and otherwise obtaining mental culture.[5]

Separately, the arrival of the Colliers was reported by George Atkinson:

We like their appearance. Mr. C. looks professional. He is needed in the Institution & we rejoice that he has come. The school opens prosperously, 25 or 30 in the College and Prep. Departments.

All three will find enough to do to keep up the classes. Prof. C. says you will secure the amount, he doubts not, for while your present subns. are conditioned, we trust you will reach the original amount proposed, $50,000....

Mrs. H. Clark died a few weeks since. [George] Durham has all the family down at the mill – what support they have I know not - but fear it is meager.

Money has been scarce this season. Now the shipments are better.[6]

Atkinson's letter suggests that the Clark family did not had an easy time after Harvey Clark's death.

The son, James Harvey, at 17 years of age ran away to join the Union Army and was never heard from. The family felt he had probably died in action.

Fortunately, George Durham, a college student who had fallen in love with the Clark daughter, Satira, was able to take the family to his family home nearby in their time of grief.

There are no records at this time as to the college's or trustees' concern for the Clarks' welfare, but there are suggestions that Mrs. Clark became depressed because there was so little to live on as the years passed. She felt the college might have helped, since her husband had been so generous.[7]

Atkinson wrote to President Marsh on February 4, 1867, again expressing the financial pressures they were facing.

---

5   *Ibid.*
6   *Ibid.*

The school goes on well so far as we hear. My chief anxiety now is for funds. We are behind, even if interest were paid up, but some of that is back, as money is very hard to be got.

Your bro & wife are expected to come out in the spring. If so you must be sure to get funds enough. A man here without money is a failure in several senses.

Possibly you design your bro for the female department. If so the prospect will be more favorable. That department supports Mrs. Reasoner very well as I understand.

Your truly

G.H. Atkinson[8]

It was difficult to run a college on the West Coast while raising the necessary monies for it in the East, and the pressures experienced by President Marsh were severe.

Alanson Hinman, a member of the Board of Trustees and proprietor of a store just south of campus, had been in charge of Jason Lee's mission at the Dalles in earlier years. Now he wrote to President Marsh with more news of church and school.

Dear Sir:

Mr. Collier is well liked by all the students and will be useful in building up the institution. He is different from Mr. Harpending who is not well calculated to get along well with the boys.

The school has been doing very well in the main. I have little or no complaint. The number in attendance at the college building is about 50, I think.

About Mrs. Reasoner in the female department – Six months pregnant,

---

7   From various sources it was learned that Mrs. Clark was partially crippled and in poor health in her later years. She could well have been worried as the years passed, although there may have been financial help we are unaware of.

8   Marsh Collection.

should not teach beyond this term. (Three months more to this term.)

I hope Mr. Miles [the Congregational minister] will take the school and teach it next term.

Mr. Miles is a pleasant gentleman and a man of good ability, I think. I hope the Church will yet have peace.[9]

This time the College needed help from the church through the use of its minister as a temporary teacher. Hinman continued that money was tight, closing with these insights into the economy: "Business is not good. Wheat is only worth out here 50 to 60 cts per bushel. Oats 25 cts. Farmer feed poor. We must have *railroads* or abandon the country. Let Oregon become connected by rail directly with the east and we are all right."

Mrs. Marsh received the aforementioned letter from Joseph Fish, dated two days later, in which he described the interior of the new building. His letter continued with news about student activities:

Our sociables are very interesting as well as instructive. They are in the college building once in three weeks. We would be very glad if you were here to take part in the sociables.

The tin pan and boiler bands have about retired from active service as their instruments have become old and need repairs and their pay is so small they can hardly afford to keep up the band and pay expenses.[10]

Joseph Fish's letter brought to mind the campus and students, as well as their activities, that she had missed. A letter sent from Mrs. Lyman to Mrs. Marsh on February 25 echoed the student's report and alluded also to the difficulties:

....As to school matters the Seminary has prospered. The girls generally have been more studious & much more serious than for several winters past.... Mr. Lyman has had a hard winter. The neighbors say he shows the marks of it in his looks. I fear sometimes he will break down when the year is through. He

---

9   *Ibid.*
10   *Ibid.*

is in school all day and much of the time busy until 11-12 [o'clock] at night. The extra labors of this added to what was before, *too much* more than he ought to do.

Our new minister [Mr. Miles] has been with us a week. We like him very much. He is finely educated, has good sermons & is very unassuming in his manners & what is more seems possessed of an excellent spirit. I trust he will be a long blessing to the church.

We have had the sociables as usual, have met at the College, as there were too many to meet in private homes.

The juniors and seniors have had the Public Speaking as last winter. The last was last week. They did very well. Mr. Miles was warm in his commendation.

We hope you will be prospered & return home before another year.

Affectionately your friend

M.D. Lyman[11]

Besides pledges and money received, Marsh had been fortunate in receiving a donation of paper, a useful commodity at the growing College. It was to be shipped by March 20, 1867.

By mid-April, the financial support Marsh received totaled $25,000, with a pledge for an additional $25,000 from Sidney E. Morse, brother of Samuel F.B. Morse, inventor of the telegraph. It must have been a relief to President Marsh to pick up his family—which now included the baby born recently in Ohio—and on May 20 begin their trip home.

The campus was a welcome sight and the children were exuberant to be home among their friends. Lyman was relieved of the responsibility of acting president, and Marsh was anxious to get back to his teaching schedule.

It was good news to learn that 1866 had seen three graduating from the college, with another three students to be graduated at the end of 1867. The succession of graduations would be a continuing process now, with ten students graduating in one of those years—1878—under Marsh's presidency.

---

11   *Ibid.* These last two letters were reminders to Mrs. Marsh of the student activities she missed.

Much was made of graduation now. The ceremonies were held in the Congregational Church, decorated for the occasion. A formal program used the seniors and music was furnished by the choral group from the college.[12]

Other milestones in the college's history were being set at this time. David Rafferty, who later received his doctorate, became the first student to take the Scientific Course at the College and graduate, in 1867, and Harriet Hoover became the first woman to take the women's three-year course of study and receive a Mistress of Science degree in 1869.[13]

In September of the year of his return to the Grove, President Marsh also received a confirmation of his request for paid transportation to New York for two of the recent graduates. The Pacific Steamship Co. agreed to provide passage from San Francisco to New York for Myron Eells, class of '66, and J. Elkanah Walker, '67. The Presbyterian minister in New York who had made arrangements wrote: "It gives me great pleasure to be able to do any service to the sons of such good missionaries as [Elkanah] Walker and [Cushing] Eells."[14]

One of the joys experienced by President Marsh upon his return was the reunion with his brother Joseph, who had arrived to take up the teaching post. It was Mrs. Joseph Marsh's first meeting with Lizzie and her children.

At this time, President Marsh also decided that it was time for his first son, Wheelock, who was four, to begin learning Latin. Wheelock describes the experience in his reminiscences:

This may throw some light on my father's scholastic and classical ideas: I am four years old (nearly five). I have learned to read simple English. To my father, it is high time I was learning Latin, if I am to be a scholar, which he presupposes. In my father's study I am set to work on McClintock and Crook's Latin Grammar. It is not for me to say it was not the best for my purpose, but I can say it was not well adapted to attract and interest my four year old mind, but I dug away with it and surprisingly derived, no doubt, some idea of language. There were vowels and consonants, amongst other new things, to learn about. Of course it helped me much in my study of Latin later in Academy and College.

---

12   James Wheelock Marsh, reminiscences.
13   Robertson, J.R.
14   Marsh Collection.

Once, I remember, Uncle Joseph came into the study where I was reciting Latin, and framed a sentence to my father in Latin, asking him if I could go over to his house to play. I understood enough to get the meaning, and was highly satisfied to hear an affirmative reply. But a long time I was kept at this, when, perhaps, I should have been outdoors playing. But such were the rigid ideas of the times.[15]

President Marsh may have appeared to be a stern classicist, probably because his parents and background reflected strong academic achievement, but he was remarkably ahead of his times in his social vision for the college. This was shown again in 1869. That year he changed his mind about segregation of the sexes and separate education for men and women. He abandoned his policy of separating academy and college, and establishing a seminary for young women. Women were admitted to regular college classes, and a three-year course of study was created for the Mistress of Science degree. The first woman to take the four-year college course and receive a Bachelor of Arts degree was Ella Scott, in 1873.[16]

October 1869 saw President Marsh leave on his third trip to the East to secure financial support for the college. Pacific was growing and this meant an expanding faculty. Joseph Marsh had been placed in charge of Ancient Languages (Latin and Greek) and head of the growing library. He could also be counted on to teach in other fields as necessary and had agreed to shoulder the duties of acting president in Sidney Marsh's absence.

In spite of the planning which had taken place, anxious letters followed the President. They described situations that were difficult to handle from the East, and some were disturbing.

A man named C.A. Huntington came out to the Grove after a meeting he attended in Portland. He was, apparently, filled with ideas and talked at great length with Prof. Collier and Prof. Joseph Marsh about what he saw as a much-needed boarding house on campus. *If* the college would raise the money for a building, he would be willing to come and manage it, he stated.

---

15   James Wheelock Marsh, reminiscences. When the Marshes returned from the East and met Uncle Joseph's family, there was a dilemma to face. Joseph had a son, James, as did Sidney. A townsman suggested one might be called Jimmy. That didn't sound like a solution, so James Wheelock became known as Wheelock in his campus days, and so continued among his friends.

16   Robertson, J.R.

Also, *if* President Marsh could finish the North College building, and then build a house worth $4,000 or $5,000 for him and his family "on an eligible site near by," he could also do some preaching as well.

He elaborated on how much the college would prosper under his ideas and management. The message covered several pages of advice, and he added that he also had sent a communication to the *Oregonian* telling of his proposals and how another teacher in the academy was needed to share the responsibilities of the overworked academy director.[17]

We have no further data on Huntington, whether he was a Congregationalist or who he might represent.

Also, a letter from Senator Corbett in Washington, D.C., on December 15, 1869, sharpened the question of a proper recognition of the $25,000 Morse gift to the college. Marsh had known Rev. Morse, a minister, and his sons, Sidney and Samuel. All three were generous. Gifts both given and pledged raised the question of how to recognize this beneficence. One suggestion was that the college might take the Morse name for its university, or it might be called Pacific and Morse University. Marsh was equally anxious to avoid slighting the Morse family, whose members certainly did not give their generous gifts expecting special honors. Senator Corbett's letter was very helpful in deciding the question:

> About changing the name in the constitution I fear there may be some
> trouble to accomplish that.... I think a "Scientific Department" called the
> Morse Professorship might be satisfactory.[18]

In New York, Sidney Marsh wrote to his wife about his campaign for funds:

Dec. 20, 1869

Dearest Lizzie:

I consider myself as certainly through, although there is some deficiency yet. But Dr. Adams told me this A.M. that he would raise the rest for me after New Years.

---

17   Marsh Collection.

18   *Ibid.*

Mr. Morse gives us $10,000 *certainly* & I think will make it $50,000.

My coming has been a great success - but the time I long for my wife and children.

I shall have no objection to its being known now that I have raised $20,000 & $10,000 at least, more not available just now.

Your Sidney[19]

Fortunately, among all the friends made in the East, there was one who was truly concerned about President Marsh as an individual. This was A.S. Hatch, of the firm Fisk & Hatch, Bankers. He reminded Marsh that the previous trip east he had provided money for teachers' salaries. Now something must be done for Marsh for the protection of his wife and children. He proposed setting up a presidential endowment, and he would raise the money himself from friends. This was much appreciated by Marsh. Hatch then proceeded to raise the endowment fund, making a generous personal contribution to set the fund in motion.[20]

May 5, 1870, saw the annual meeting of the Board of Trustees of the University, who had a lengthy agenda of items for decision or information. The trustees were pleased with the report Dr. Marsh gave of his successful eastern trip, as he gave an accounting of the $20,000 raised and the Presidential endowment fund being raised by Mr. Hatch. Since the second eastern trip had produced funds to guarantee faculty salaries, it now appeared Pacific had established a solid financial foundation of gifts and pledges.

A resolution for the "Land committee, Prest. Marsh and Prof. Lyman, to subdivide our lots, so as to make three lots of one" was accepted. Where originally the lots had been a full acre in size, it was now felt that smaller lots would be more feasible.

The next resolution touched on the fact that it was time to recognize Oregon's need for public schools—a free universal education for all children. There had been arguments about this matter, as some settlers said, "Where I came from you paid for your own children's education." The

19   *Ibid.*
20   *Ibid.*

rebuttal was, "But this is America, and we believe every child is entitled to an education to be paid for by taxes." Oregon, therefore, began setting up school districts and the resolution voted on by the Board followed this pattern: "Resolved, to sell the Academy & one lot to the district for a free school without its furniture upon the terms recommended by the faculty."

The resolution that followed was detailed: "The funds from the sale of the Academy be applied to fit up Academical rooms in the new college building & pay deficit of $165.67 to Prof. Anderson."[21]

Whether the above resolutions were implemented immediately is unclear, as well as what building was to be sold. It might have been the "den," as Scott called it when a student at Pacific, which could accommodate 15 to 20 students. The Academy on campus would continue the education of the older student group.

Other resolutions followed, including one that "the appointment of an assistant to the Academy be left to the faculty." This seems to have been the first year the faculty would be responsible for specifics of this sort. Up to this time, Marsh had been responsible for faculty assignments, which were ratified by the Trustees.

The resolution about the much-needed boarding house was presented at this meeting, "that the Prest. be requested to make any arrangement deemed needful for a Boarding House." Until now, students lived with local families, paying board and room while attending school if they lived too far from Forest Grove for daily commuting. Some found simple living accommodations where they could cook. A good many of the boys trudged on foot to the Grove early Monday morning, carrying their five-day supply of food, as well as books, and staying in rooms where they could take care of themselves. Then, they headed home for the weekend of farm work, and repeated the trip on Monday.

The immediate decisions were now completed, and were followed by two specific interests on the agenda. News had come of the death of Rev. Theron Baldwin, Secretary for the Society for the Promotion of Collegiate Education at the West. He had been actively promoting Pacific University since its birth. Five resolutions dealt with the Trustees' acceptance of the news, sending "a resolution each to family, educational office," and lastly, "Resolved that the Trustees desire to procure a portrait or life sized Photograph of Dr. Baldwin to be placed in the Library Room of the Institution."

---

21   Records of the Board of Trustees.

The next resolutions emphasized gratitude to the Morse family, particularly Sidney Morse, Esq. of New York, whose "interest and funds given and proposed, to endow a Christian College in the Pacific border of our Great Republic" are a "memento of the liberality and noble aims of the donor."

A third: "Resolved that the Trustees would be happy to receive and place in our library a portrait or life size Photograph of Mr. Sidney E. Morse and his honored father, late minister in Charlestown, Ms. and also his eminent brother, Prof. S.F.B. Morse."

Finally: "Resolved that the Board present our thanks to Prof. S.F.B. Morse for his generous gift of telegraphic apparatus to our Institution." The telegraphic apparatus remains today in the museum at Old College Hall.

This concluded the amenities and apparently covered all bases on which the Trustees were to vote. The College appreciated particularly the Morse contributions, knowing it represented the largest collective gift to the college up to 1870. Rev. Morse at the time of his death made an added bequest to Pacific which could not come until after Mrs. Morse's death.

The responsibility for the boarding house was on the President's shoulders, and Wheelock Marsh's reminiscences describe the action that followed:

> It was in the 1870's that my father built the three story house, designed for a boarding house for students. Such a house had come to be almost a necessity for the school, and as the college could not build it, my father did. It was an addition, his house standing as an ell to the north. The responsibility of managing such a house, inevitably fell upon my mother; but she always had a competent woman employed to supposedly carry this load.[22]

Finally, the boarding house was finished and ready for occupancy. According to Wheelock Marsh's memory, it housed many students from areas further removed from Forest Grove. His reminiscence continued:

> I remember being with us, Eugene and Herbert McCormack of Eugene; Zenas Moody, son of the Governor; Fred Stump, son of the river steamboat captain; Lulu Donnell of the Dalles. I think it was maintained till about the time Herrick Hall was built. Discontinued, the two houses were sawn asunder, and the original house moved some 50 feet north, turned quarter way round, and now is Walker Hall.

---

22   James Wheelock Marsh, reminiscences.

As the year 1870 drew to its close, the world moved closer to the West Coast in an unexpected way. Commodore Perry had opened the doors of Japan to the world. The Japanese immediately saw opportunities beyond their own shores. Many began to find their way to San Francisco, looking for education, wanting to learn English and hoping to learn more about the new world.

Data from George Haskell Marsh, Wheelock's brother, sheds some light on Marsh's intense interest, and is included in Wheelock's recollections:

> I am glad to find that my brother, George Haskell, has some knowledge of it [Japanese students], and understanding the quality of his mind, am sure of it. His information was that our father met these boys by some chance, in San Francisco, they, unsettled as to their future.[23]

On June 1, 1870, Sidney Marsh received a letter from Sato Momoturo, a 16-year-old Japanese youth living in San Francisco. In it, the boy explains he has written to his father in Japan about coming to Pacific, but would not come until he heard from his father. Since he was employed with a Japanese company in San Francisco, he said he could stay where he was for a time and find other young men to send to Pacific University.

He wrote again to Marsh September 5, affording an insight into his background and the meaning of the new opportunities in America:

> I left Japan when I was 14 years old (I am now 17 years old in Jap. but 16 in American) so I can not know much of our country's manner or condition but since I come here, I have much enjoyed and become wiser, in my idea & often recognize the poor circumstance of our country, but were I in home surely, I can not see much idea as this, and supposed all time my country the best, believe me, I am not to proud myself.... My Grand father & father are now physicians. They had been educated by Dutch physicians in Nagasake where you know many years before Caodore Perly [Commodore Perry] first cruised into the harbour of Gedo or Yedo [Tokyo], now in the bay of Yokohama. They, my fathers through their education came home from Nagasaki & G. father first taught scolars, & after father, now G. father is in Yokohama, when I went to Yokohama I was 12 years old and I was taught by Mrs. Hepburn wife of an American doctor M. who made Jap. and Eng.

---

23   *Ibid.*

Dictionary & now he has translating Holy Scripture, I heard he has almost finished. Then I was imployed in Yokohama by Matzo & Co. now I am.

1 or 2 Colleges have now been built in Yedo, but I do not know why Government let not every person go. Mostly high ranked people's young to what we called 2 sworded fellows [samurai]. And so many poor youngs can not go, if they have mind, they will have any chance to go, I think at present Government let them go, any person, but they are ignorent, and yet many are dispise European Science, of cause they do not know which way is America or China. At least we want 64 Colleges in all parts of Japan. There are 64 States what we called. As I wrote you last by Tamura [the student sent to Pacific by Momoturo] that almost every thing is completed but in miserly have not yet good education or the light in night. And so many people do not consider any resons in, often high ranks and do not make agree one another only make themselves as high & is igurlent.... It is I think pretty hard or need of patience for a person to do good for our country at present.

We're very much interested that many feringers [foreigners] who are willing to educate us, this is what we should need. I am gladly satisfied in your last letter that you can educate a few at your own place....

I will write you again, perhaps many meanings in this will not express what I mean, then ask to Tamura, he may be able to tell you & obliged.

Truly yours
Sato Momoturo
at Japanese Store
San Francisco, Cal.[24]

On September 21, Sato Momoturo wrote to Marsh regarding two more prospective Japanese students:

Bearer Saito and Nosey are my countrymen. I hope you will find they are good boys and hope you will try until the next May and then if they have kept their service and learn faithfully it is more than we wish, but if they do not learn, please do not keep them any longer. I will try to repay you their expenses.

---

24   Marsh Collection.

We think more of our countrymen will come here in a few months. I thought it is better for them to come here though they have not money. I wrote telling them it is better to come here to learn Foreign manner than to stay with ignorants in their present circumstances.[25]

That same day, a letter was sent to Marsh from Louis R. Lull which confirmed Sato Momoturo's information. Lull's letterhead was Hall of the Society of California Pioneers, which suggests that he may have been the one who interested Marsh in the Japanese students.

Your of the 9th inst with $25 L.T. came duly. Conferring with Memo Sato, I concluded it best to send you Saito and Gosa. They had only $20 joint money. My friend, Wm. Norris, Esq, of the Steamship Co., after reading Tamara's letter to Memo, put their joint passage at $25 L.T. coin $22.20, a reduction of the regular fare of $18.60. I think this may be credited to Tamara's letter & the taking appearance of Memo with whom Mr. Norris was much pleased.

I trust they may all please you & that you may live to see the day when this seed you have planted shall bring forth an hundred fold, blessing leaves for the healing of the nation in darkness.

Yours in haste
Louis R. Lull[26]

It is fortunate that a postscript to Lull's letter alerted Dr. Marsh as to the time of arrival, because Sato Momaturo was sending his letter for personal delivery by the students upon their arrival in Forest Grove.

The Japanese students arrived, eager to learn. They were enrolled in the program to meet their needs, and became part of the Marsh household. This interested young Wheelock, and his report shed some more light on their life:

---

25 *Ibid.*
26 *Ibid.* The fact that Japanese students found their way to Oregon and Pacific was gratifying in the broadened experiences it brought to both the students and the community.

The Japanese boys lived with us, working for their board and going to school at the Academy. Two of them, Hatatara Tamara and Kimpay Saito, remained with us through Academy and College. Agero Nosea went to the home of Uncle Pro. Joseph Marsh where he likewise remained. These boys were studious, and anxious to learn all about America.

My mother called attention to the fact that Saito used to stand his spelling book up on the sink before him while he washed dishes, to lose no time studying. Tamara was rugged, alert in body and mind; Saito, more frail; while Nosea always seemed to me flabby.

My father employed Tamara and Saito, with Bert and Rees Leabo, neighbor boys to "slash" several acres of fir trees on the land he had near Newberg. The boys camped together and it must have been an experience for them.[27]

Tamara, with the other two boys, graduated from college in the class of 1876, with E.M.L. Atkinson and Ella Watt.

Tamara wound up his college course brilliantly. He had acquired a good command of English, the Latin (required then even in the Scientific Course) having helped him a great deal.

---

27   James Wheelock Marsh, reminiscences.

Chapter 12
Progress into the Future: 1871-1879

Forest Grove began to grow as the westward move continued, although not as fast as the "land committee" of the Trustees had hoped. The name Forest Grove appeared on a map of Oregon made by John B. Preston, the first surveyor general of Oregon on October 21, 1851. The town was not incorporated until 1871, although Articles of Government were established from the beginning as they were needed.

This form of community organization was a necessity from the beginning, not an artificial exercise in bureaucracy. As early as 1860, for example, Alanson Hinman penned a note to Alvin Smith, the district magistrate, complaining about dogs killing his sheep. He ended the note, stating, "If we must wait for a person to *see* the killing we might end up raising dogs, not sheep."

Two years after incorporation, the town had its first election. In 1877, Prof. Joseph Marsh, Dr. Marsh's brother and the college librarian, was elected President of the Town Trustees.

Twenty years later, the words "Mayor" and "City Council" were introduced.

Forest Grove's genesis as a town was not unique to Western development, although its underpinnings may have been especially strong because of the presence of the Academy and Pacific University. S.T. Walker, writing of this period, credits Harvey Clark as "the founder of Forest Grove and the liberal donor to Tualatin Academy and Pacific University." He goes on to describe the early town and those settlers who became part of west Tualatin Plain's growth. Part of this is incorporated in early chapters, but names of residents are added now:

In the earliest years the post office was at the residence of Mr. A.T. Smith, a little beyond where the condenser now stands. The road from Portland to Lafayette, the nearest town to the south, left the present road to Cornelius just beyond the east side of the Hinman farm.... It used to be at that time quite a chore to go to the post office but as the mail came only once a week it was not like it is when one must go two or three times a day.

In that day there were very few houses – Mr. A.T. Smith, Hon. A. Hinman, Rev. Harvey Clark, Deac. E.S. Tanner in "Yankeetown" as all south of Council Creek was called. Deac. F.G. Naylor, west of town, Henry Buxton, Sr. and H. Buxton, Jr., and Benjamin Catching to the northwest; Orus Brown, Alvin Brown and George Beal to the north, and William Stokes and William Catching to the east, Mr. Black, R.M. Porter, William Rafferty, George Spencer, David Harrell, Milton Tuttle, Rev. C. Eells, Mr. Keeler in the town proper.... Prof. E.D. Shattuck (academy faculty) built the house which stands on the block east of the Christian church.[1]

Stores began to appear just south of the campus. There was Fearnside and Bowlby, a general store, A. Hinman's mercantile store and Samuel Hughes' blacksmith shop facing the east corner of the campus.

As the town grew, progress at the college was being measured in the increased number of students from outlying communities and the need for additions to the faculty. Yet Marsh was bothered by the slowness of growth in the student body and still-small number of graduates each spring. These same students, however, went out after graduation and became leaders in their chosen fields and brought credit to Pacific University.

In spite of the frustratingly slow growth in population, the college's curriculum and faculty expanded to meet the needs of the student body. Prof. Joseph Marsh, who taught Ancient Languages and was Librarian, was solid in his teaching and valuable in many ways beyond his duties. Prof. Alexander Anderson, who had been in charge of the Academy, was transferred to the College in 1872 to teach Mathematics. He also added a new course, "The Art of Teaching," which in later years would become part

---

1   Walker, S.T., writing to the local newspaper at a later date, said Deacon Tanner lived in Yankeetown and Naylor to the west. The land claim of Naylor was south of the present Pacific Avenue, but also west of the Smith and Clark claims.

of the teaching in normal, or teaching training, schools. Unfortunately, he stayed only two years, leaving the campus in 1874.

The Science Department of the College had Prof. Taft as its first instructor, in 1861. Since that beginning, it grew to include Prof. George H. Collier in 1867, who came to teach Chemistry, Biology, Geology and Mathematics. In 1872, Thomas Condon returned to Forest Grove to deliver a lecture on geology and his discoveries. He was now ready to accept Marsh's invitation to join the Pacific faculty in 1873, teach Geology and help lighten Prof. Collier's teaching load.

These were knowledgeable men who brought strength to the College. Yet, undercurrents began to intrude on the well-ordered campus. President Marsh began to sense a dominance on the part of Prof. Collier and possibly a few of the faculty. Echoes that a group of Presbyterians were willing to take over Pacific reached President Marsh and disturbed him greatly.

In May 1873, Marsh wrote to a minister friend in the East for advice, telling him of the uncertainty he felt and questioning how it should be handled. His good friend W.G.T. Shedd, who had been helpful in raising money during Marsh's visits, answered with thoughtful possibilities:

> 148 E. 38th N.Y.
> May 22, 1873

Rev. S.H. Marsh. D.D.

Dear Sir

If your college faculty was a harmonious body, there could not be a doubt, I think, that you should remain where you are for the following reasons.

1. You will do more for the cause of Christ & his Church as a teacher than as a preacher.

2. A transfer of yourself & family to the East at your age would be accompanied with many sacrifices and discouragements. The East is over crowded & churches call a man of forty-five an "old man." You have a right and a duty to look out for the future of your six children. You can educate them better at less expense than you can in the East.

3. You say you "could acquiesce in a decision of a majority of the faculty & go along & draw your salary" or you could enter a contest. You must

decide...but I should incline to the former as the best way to succeed in the end. You are disappointed that the College has no more students and is restricted in its influence. This is no fault of yours.

4. Perhaps in the changes that may go on something more desirable may be opened to you in Oregon. Should the line be drawn between the Presbyterians & Congregationalists and a new College be proported [proposed?] by the former, you might have a new field offered to you.

....My advice is to stay where you are & do the work at your hand, until Providence points out another. I would *not* go East & look up a pastoral charge.

Yours sincerely

W.G.T. Shedd[2]

This advice was helpful, though it was not a solution to the problem Sidney Marsh had to face and settle.

With the year 1875 approaching, it was necessary to plan another trip to the East, and Marsh set off on his fourth trip back east with worries that made the trip less enjoyable than on previous occasions. The college and faculty problems disturbed him, making concentration on financial subscriptions difficult.

A letter to Mrs. Marsh in early 1875 showed his thinking about the future:

My dear wife

For several days my mind has been upon this plan –

To get the Trustees to take my house, furniture & all at say $4000 or $4500, & have you all come east – perhaps if I can make arrangements for the

---

2   Marsh Collection. A year or two earlier, Marsh had a friend in Newberg who was so anxious to have a college that he begged Dr. Marsh to come and found a school for his community. He was willing to give a parcel of land for a campus. Sidney Marsh did not accept the invitation, feeling his work at Pacific was not completed. That was an easier decision to make than this present dilemma.

children in Ohio – then have you & the baby here with me. I need to have
the *cheer* & comfort of having you with me – but one important reason is
that it makes it possible for me to go to Or. without disclosing my
determination to have a Trustees meeting & settle some things which it is not
politic for me to talk about before hand. – Hinman & Joseph may understand
what I expect to do – another reason is that it disposes of my property, etc.,

& relieves part of the embarrassment in case I wish to remain here.[3]

He concluded the letter by mentioning the will of Rev. Morse and the anticipated bequest of about $25,000, noting "If I should leave the institution this
would all be lost." He closed, saying, "I wish it were possible for you to fix
up, shut up the house & come on bag & baggage."

The problem continued to weigh on him throughout his stay in the East.
In a birthday greeting to his wife on August 28, he expressed his love and
the blessing of his family. He then stated:

I am feeling a little blue at the prospects of a fight over the question at issue
with C. I sometimes feel like quietly getting out of the way, and letting

Collier have full sway. I shall wait till I hear from Hinman & Joseph.[4]

With Joseph Marsh serving as acting president and Alanson Hinman now
chairman of the Board of Trustees, there were two strong and dependable
men whose judgment could be counted upon. The letter Mrs. Marsh
received a month later relieved her mind somewhat.

Sept. 18, 1875

My much beloved wife –

I received a letter from Mr. Hinman which he closed with these words which
have done me much good. "Have courage. I think your wife has. I believe
you will remain President of the Institution and bless it as you always have."

I called upon Rev. – last evening more particularly to talk about what I could

---

3   *Ibid.*
4   *Ibid.*

honorably and consistently do among Presbyterians with the certainty that we are to stand in the acknowledged position that I claim for the Institution, i.e. that we are under no control, direct or implied, secret or open, of the Congregational body. I think I can go honestly to Presbyterians for help.

I don't care to stir up the matter now. Condon is very sensitive about it, but I am satisfied if the fact is established as I think it is.

Probably it may be best to stay till well into the winter. Am a little uncertain whether it is best to return & meet the issue with C. [Collier] now before he has time to machinate more or wait until the college year is nearly through so that C. can more easily leave as I think he must.[5]

Ten days later, Marsh wrote to his wife again, suggesting that she might sell the house to the trustees and bring the family east. Then he could stay in the East and raise money and preach. He ended the letter clearly expressing his personal need: "I am almost desperate. It requires all my resolution to stay here in this way."[6]

This may have contributed to his decisiveness in cutting his eastern trip short, leaving the financial campaign unfinished and returning to Oregon. There, he made his position clear, stating that a group of faculty had suggested the Presbyterians would like to take over Pacific University, and this could not be done. Pacific had been founded by Congregationalists, with a Board of Trustees and was chartered by the state as such. Pacific University would not be sold or given to another denominational group. The Trustees and the President stood together.

There the matter was dropped. If there had been an implied threat that a rival college would be built near Pacific, it did not materialize.

An early history of the College, written by Prof. James Rood Robertson in 1905, notes the tides of new pressures which lapped at the college:

---

5   *Ibid.* Sidney Harper Marsh had been such a strong president and so knowledgeable in educational programs that it is hard to understand his apparent vacillation seen in this letter to his wife. Actually, he was not weak, but carefully weighing the pros and cons of the situation he faced while so many miles from home.

6   *Ibid.*

As the administration of President Marsh drew to a close a difference of policy, which had existed for some time previous, became more prominent. Some of the trustees and friends of the college were desirous that a closer relation be established between the college and the Congregational Church, and proposed that the association of ministers and churches of the Congregational body elect the proportion of trustees allowed to that denomination rather than that they be elected by the board itself, as the charter provided. The difference was one of those honest differences of opinion which are always likely to occur and have occurred in so many religious institutions in regard to the same question, but it was unfortunate in its effect in that it led to divided councils where unity of aim was best calculated to insure permanence for the work promised for the immediate future. It also added greatly to the burdens of President Marsh, who was opposed to the plan, and together with his delicate constitution and a life of hard work caused his breakdown.[7]

The Congregational Association, led surprisingly by George Atkinson, moved in to protect its school, demanding a larger part in choosing trustees and setting the policies of education. Marsh was adamant about this request, which had been introduced earlier. He patiently repeated, as he had done previously, that the college was built independent of the control of any church body in spite of the fact that the original trustees were strongly representative of the Congregational, Baptist and Presbyterian denominations. It received money from a variety of sources, individuals and church groups besides Congregationalists, and its student body was open to all who wanted to come. It must remain independent and beyond sectarian control.

Marsh did remind the Congregational body that the Board of Trustees selected its members very carefully, with a certain proportion being Congregationalists. They also chose representatives of various businesses and interests to give a balance to their thinking on educational matters.

Alanson Hinman, chairman, was firm in his support of Marsh. While a few trustees were willing to accept the wishes of the denominational body, Hinman stood firm and prevented sectarian control from defeating the independence of the school.

The problem was alleviated with the departure of Professors Collier and Condon. At that time, President Marsh asked Capt. R. Lamson to join the faculty, and for one year Lamson taught Mathematics, until William N.

---

7   Robertson, J.R

Ferrin arrived the following year to take over the department. Prof. Ferrin was a fellow Vermonter and well prepared for his work at the young college. He served many years on the faculty and later was appointed president of Pacific.

Prof. Ferrin was a bachelor when he came to Forest Grove, but before long, Mrs. Marsh suggested he visit at her parents' home in Ohio. This served to introduce him to her sister Martha, or Mattie as she was known. The suggestion bore fruit, for in the 1880s Prof. Ferrin brought Martha to Forest Grove as his wife, much to Elizabeth's joy.[8]

Joseph Marsh and William Ferrin gave strength to the college. They had a sense of commitment and a staying quality which the growing college needed, and they firmly believed in President Marsh's policies. This gave a feeling of relief to a man suffering physically from poor health—later determined to be tuberculosis—and spiritually from others who were trying to circumvent him in such trying ways at a time when the school could least stand it.

In spite of his worries about Pacific, President Marsh's active mind was at work, and the redwood trees planted in the area around Forest Grove are one result of his action. They are described in Wheelock Marsh's reminiscences:

> My brother distinctly remembers the planting of them by our father and
> Uncle Joseph; it was about the year 1876. Those trees about Forest Grove
> and the court house yard in Hillsboro are the gigantean species of sequoia,
> the "big trees" of California. They were introduced here by the Porter
> nursery, east of the Alvin Brown place north of town.[9]

After the spring term was concluded in 1877, Marsh decided to go to the Hood River area, hoping the climate might clear the pressure on his lungs and improve his health. He took his son, Wheelock, then aged 15, with him for support.

In Wheelock's words:

---

8   Marsh, J.W., reminiscences. Prof. Ferrin was valuable as an educator, and also a strong and dependable individual.

9   *Ibid.* Those of us who have over the years admired the sequoia trees, planted in pairs, may find it interesting as to how they came to be planted out of their natural environment.

My father had gone to Hood River in the first attempt at change of climate for health recovery. He had taken me with him – the trip from Portland was then made by steamboat, with portage over the Cascade rapids. We built a small rough cabin at the foot of a bluff, down which a small creek tumbled. Here we lived, walking up a trail a quarter of a mile to Mr. & Mrs. E. L. Smith's for our meals. Mr. Smith had recently moved there from Olympia, Wash. for the benefit of his health, a tubercular condition.[10]

Wheelock was suffering from frequent attacks of ague and was not in the best condition himself to care for his father, but he could give companionship. That helped Mrs. Marsh, staying at home with the younger children.

Shortly after they had settled into the quiet relaxation of the cabin, Marsh reported to Wheelock that a man had come from Camas Prairie looking for a teacher for their new school. Smith and Marsh had talked it over and decided that Wheelock would be a good teacher for the new school. They had even settled the matter without asking Wheelock's opinion. Wheelock was "violently opposed," he said; he wasn't well himself, and "Camas Prairie was twenty miles from the Columbia River, at the foot of Mt. Adams."

Frazier, the school director, arrived at the Marsh cabin a few days later, as Wheelock stated:

...to get me, and the next day we left, I accoutered in a long ministerial coat of my father's, oversized overalls rolled up at the bottom, a nondescript hat, but carrying my father's valuable watch. But people there seemed to pay no attention to one's clothes.[11]

They arrived at the foot of Mt. Adams two days later and Wheelock recognized its "overwhelming grandeur." Another trip, to Goldendale, was necessary to get a teaching certificate which was duly issued for teaching first and second grades. In this way, Wheelock Marsh, aged fifteen, began his teaching of twelve children in a floorless log school room.

---

10   *Ibid.* In spite of illness, Sidney Marsh had his young son's welfare on his mind. Even more important, he saw an isolated community with a school that needed a teacher, and felt both objectives could be met.

11   *Ibid.*

In spite of his being alone in a strange place, the summer teaching went well enough. After one bout with ague, he was surprisingly cured by a dose of medicine. After receiving a letter from Wheelock expressing his loneliness, Marsh borrowed a horse and came to see his son. Instead of staying just one day, he remained three days, sleeping at night on hay in a barn and eating meals at neighborhood homes. From then on, Wheelock was content and decided he might return for the next season's teaching. He said his certificate was for two years and he must use it up.

When the summer ended, the Marshes went back to Forest Grove for the college year. This also marked a return to formal Sunday services. And Sunday, as Wheelock described it, was a very distinct part of the culture at Pacific:

> Frivolity and play on Sunday were frowned upon. When my father was home I spent many Sabbath (as he called it) afternoons learning extracts from the Bible and hymns. Religion in the college too had a positive place: attendance at church service was required, and chapel every morning. When home on Sunday my father conducted a service for college students on Sunday afternoons.[12]

President Marsh, even with his health problem, kept his dream for Pacific alive and active by example as well as teaching. One of his favorite sayings was "Respect yourself and others will respect you." An objective in the educational process, he stated, was "to develop *Men*, not merely scholars."[13]

A second summer was spent at Hood River, in 1878. While Wheelock used up his teaching certificate, Sidney Marsh had to admit there was little improvement in his health. At summer's end, the Marshes, father and son, again returned to Forest Grove and the family. There, Sidney Marsh and his beloved Lizzie faced the inevitable signs of his mortality together, although there was always hope as long as there was life. One more trip to California might bring improvement, he felt. First, he told Wheelock that he needed

---

12   *Ibid.* Back home for the beginning of the fall semester, Marsh not only taught and supervised the total program, but recognized Sunday as a special day of the week and of utmost importance in building individual character.

13   *Ibid.* James Wheelock Marsh, an understanding son in his father's final years, became much closer than happens in many father-son relationships. The devotion he felt is marked by his trip to California.

the youth's help. Wheelock's answer was a word of assurance, and his reminiscences tell it vividly:

> Before leaving for California my father had dictated to me, saying I must be his amanuensis, among other things, his final communication to the board of trustees of the college beginning: "In a few days it will be twenty-five years", finally setting forth what his objectives have been and the difficulties met, and ending *"God Bless Pacific University."*

> In the fall of 1878 he made one final attempt by going to California, taking me with him for assistance. He charged me seriously that if anything happened to him, to not let them bury him at sea.... After three weeks in San Rafael, across the bay from San Francisco, he gave up hope.

> In San Francisco, he put up at the Palace Hotel, new, and of world fame. Perhaps he wanted me to see a little of high life, of which I was densely ignorant. The hotel had a large, glass roofed patio, into which the equipages drove, and overhead the first electric light that was installed for practical illumination.

> Here my father and Mr. Failing [college treasurer] spent the evening in conversation; and Mr. Failing sent us, on our return to Portland, to his home and bedroom for comfort.

> This was about the end and my father died within about three months, early in February, 1879 [February 2nd].

> His demise cast a cloud over Forest Grove and the effect on the student body was profound, as they held their own memorial service for him in the college chapel the morning of the funeral.[14]

The Board of Trustees of Pacific University, under Alanson Hinman's leadership as President, chose Prof. Joseph Marsh as Acting President while they sought a man to fill the vacancy left by President Marsh's death.

Sidney Harper Marsh had lived to see the College on a sound footing; he had seen Oregon reach statehood. He had written often to newspapers

---

14   *Ibid.*

and influential leaders about the need for railroads in the West, and had seen the early results. (To be sure, the tracks did not pass through Forest Grove's center, but were laid south near the Carnation Mill and Smith's post office.) And the town had grown enough to have its own governing body.

President Marsh left his blessing on both Forest Grove and Pacific University. He was a true Oregon pioneer.

Epilogue

Creating a university in the heart of a wilderness is indeed a story of "splendid audacity." At many stages of Pacific University's creation, it could have disappeared except as a historical footnote. Worse, Pacific could have remained a minor institution of no great import to anyone.

However, the success of this bold venture was due to men and women like Harvey Clark, George Atkinson, Tabitha Brown, Sidney Marsh and many, many others who pursued their ideals and proved able to surpass their circumstances. In the process, these pioneers left their mark on Oregon in its transition to statehood...on the development of commerce, industry and transportation...on the culture of the Willamette Valley, Tualatin Plain and Forest Grove...and on thousands of students who in turn extended the influence of this institution.

For this, they must be remembered. Institutions are the lengthened shadows of great men and women, and they live with us still today.

Bibliography

BOOKS

Atkinson, George H., *Journal* and sections entitled *Mrs. Atkinson's Narrative*.

Atkinson, Nancy Bates, *Biography of Rev. G.H. Atkinson, D.D.*, uses his Journal and sections titled "Mrs. Atkinson's Narrative."

Cannon, Miles, *Waiilatpu* (1915), Capital News, Boise, ID.

Carey, Charles H., *A General History of Oregon* (1935), 2 vols., Metropolitan Press, Portland, OR.

Clarke, S.A., *Pioneer Days of Oregon History* (1905), vol. II, Arthur H. Clark, Glendale, CA.

DeVoto, Bernard, *Across the Wide Missouri* (1947), Houghton Mifflin Co., Boston, MA.

Dobbs, Caroline C., *Men of Champoeg* (1932), Metropolitan Press, Portland, OR.

Drury, Clifford M., *Elkanah & Mary Walker* (1940), Caxton Press, Boise, ID; *A Tepee in His Front Yard* (1949), Binford & Mort, Portland, OR; *First White Women Over the Rockies* (1963), 3 vols., Arthur Clark Publ., Glendale, CA.

Eells, Rev. Myron, *History of the Congregational Association of Oregon and Washington Territory*,1848-1880 (1881).

Fairfield, James, *Oberlin, the Colony and the College* (1883), Oberlin College Library, Oberlin, OH.

Fletcher, Robert Samuel, *History of Oberlin College*, Oberlin College Library.

157

Bibliography

Fuller, George W., *History of the Pacific Northwest* (1946), Alfred Knopf.

Gaston, Joseph, *The Centennial History of Oregon* (1912).

Gray, William H., *History of Oregon* (1870), Portland, OR.

History of St. Lawrence Co., Genealogy Room, New York City Public Library.

History of Quincy (Ill.) and Adams County, Wilcox Publ., vol. 1.

Hornell, Rev. George T., *Oberlin Student Monthly*, vol. 1 (Sept. 1859), Oberlin College Library.

Hurlbert, Archer B. & Dorothy P., *Marcus Whitman, Crusader* (1839-1947), Parts II & III – American Board letters, publ. by Stewart Commission of Colorado College and Denver Public Library (1839-1847).

Leonard, Delavan, *The Story of Oberlin*, chapter on Oberlin's Contributions to Missions.

Lockley, Fred, *Oregon Yesterdays*, Portland, OR.

Mackey, Harold, *The Kalapuyans* (1974), Mission Hill Museum Assn., Salem, OR.

Montgomery, Richard G., *The White Headed Eagle*, John McLoughlin, Builder of an Empire (1934), Macmillan Publishing Co., New York, NY.

The Oregon Archives, official printed reports of legislation (1843-1847).

Paden, Irene D., *The Wake of the Prairie Scho*oner (1947), Macmillan Publishing Co.

Richards, Lyndall, *Churches Along the Oregon Trail* (1976), Central Pacific Conference of the United Church of Christ, Portland, OR. *History of the Oregon Congregational Churches*, Forest Grove, OR.

Russell, Osborne, *Journal of a Trapper* (1914), edited from original manuscript, Coe Collection of Western Americana, Yale University Library and Oregon Historical Society.

Scott, Harvey D., *The Oregon Country*, 6 vols. (1924), Riverside Press, Cambridge, MA.

Terrell, John Upton, *Furs by Astor* (1963), Willliam Morrow & Co., New York, NY.

Victor, Frances Fuller, *All Over Oregon & Washington* (1872), John H. Carmody & Co., San Francisco, CA. *The River of the West* (1879), R.W. Bliss & Co. & R.J. Trumbull, San Francisco, CA.

White, Elijah, *Ten Years in Oregon*, Travel and Adventures West of the Rocky Mts. of Dr. E. White and Lady (1850), edited by Miss A.J. Allen, Andrus, Gauntlett & Co., Ithaca, NY, "entered according to Act of Congress 1846 by Elijah White," sub-agent of Indian Affairs.

Wislizenius, P., M.D., *A Journey to the Rocky Mountains in the Year 1839*, (1840) University of Missouri Library, Columbia, MO.

WPA Federal Writers Project, *History of Quincy, Illinois.*

PERIODICALS

Argus, Hillsboro, OR, on the dissolution of Clark-Smith Indian Mission (Oct. 13, 1927), archived with Griffin papers at Pacific University.

Oberlin College records and early cash books, 1837, archived with Mr. Love, Alumni and Treasury files.

Oregon Historical Quarterlies, "Origin of Pacific University" (1905) James Rood Robertson; G.H. Atkinson Diary (1847-1859); E. Ruth Rockwood (Sept. 1937).

The Herald Whig, Quincy, IL, The story of "God's barn" and the church, Quincy, IL.

The Vermonter; Leon Gay (March 1935), History of stone houses built by the Clark brothers in Chester, VT.

Vermont Life, Leon Gay (Autumn 1950).

OTHER SOURCES

Bancroft Library, Berkeley, Calif., manuscripts of pioneers and early settlers, Newell, Meek and Ermatinger in 1840 period; Joel Walker and others in early government.

Hammond Library, Chicago Theological Seminary, Chicago, IL, depository of the files of the Board of Home Missions from 1843, including the records, reports and letters of Harvey Clark, George Atkinson, Thomas Condon, and others.

Houghton Library, Harvard University, Cambridge, MA, depository of the American Board for Foreign Missions, including reports and correspondence between western missions and the eastern offices, 1836-1847.

Huntington Library, San Marino, CA, George Atkinson family letters and other correspondence of the 1800 period, including a fine collection of Oregon material.

Oregon Historical Society, Portland, OR, Alvin T. Smith day-by-day diary from 1820 in Connecticut to Quincy, Illinois, the Whitman Mission and Oregon; Danforth papers, collected by A.T. Smith; other collections including Eva Emery Dye's notes on Harvey Clark, A.T. Smith and other early settlers used by her as a resource for her books.

Pacific University Library, Forest Grove, OR, Emeline Cadwell Clark autograph album, 1834-1837; John S. Griffin collection of papers; Sidney Harper Marsh collection of sermons, sample subscription books, and letters, 1843-1879; Record Books of early trustees on organizing the school – Clark and Atkinson; typed copies of materials including Tabitha Brown's experiences on her trip to Oregon, Myron Eells' manuscript on the early years of Pacific, and Elizabeth Miller's information on her first year of teaching.

www.ingramcontent.com/pod-product-compliance
Lightning Source LLC
LaVergne TN
LVHW011229080426
835509LV00005B/406